Land, Conflict & Justice: Governance, Power, and Pathways to Equitable Resolution

SAFRIN SALAM

Land, Conflict & Justice: Governance, Power, and Pathways to Equitable Resolution

ELIVA PRESS

ISBN: 978-99993-3-849-3

Cover Design: Eliva Press
Cover Image: www.ingimage.com
Email: info@elivapress.com
Website: www.elivapress.com

This Eliva Press imprint is published by the registered company Eliva Press Global Ltd. part of Eliva Press S.R.L. Publishing Group

The registered company address is: Pope Hennessy Street Level 2, Hennessy Tower Port Louis, Mauritius
Eliva Press S.R.L. Publishing Group legal address is: Bd. Cuza-Voda 1/4 of. 21, Chisinau, Moldova, Europe

LAND, CONFLICT & JUSTICE: GOVERNANCE, POWER, AND PATHWAYS TO EQUITABLE RESOLUTION

BY

Dr. SAFRIN SALAM, S.H., M.H.

PREFACE

Praise be to God Almighty for His grace and guidance, which have enabled the completion of this reference book, *Land, Conflict & Justice: Governance, Power, and Pathways to Equitable Resolution*. This volume is presented as an academic contribution to a deeper and more comprehensive understanding of the intricate relationship between land, conflict, and justice within the broader frameworks of governance, power, and equitable dispute resolution.

Land is not merely an economic asset. It represents identity, livelihood, social belonging, ecological sustainability, and the material foundation of political authority. Across diverse global and local contexts, land issues have become both catalysts and reflections of structural inequality, social conflict, contested legitimacy, and tensions between formal legal systems and customary practices. To examine land, therefore, is to examine power—its distribution, negotiation, and institutionalization—within historical and contemporary processes shaped by colonial legacies, post-colonial state formation, development paradigms, and emerging technological transformations.

This reference book is structured around a coherent analytical framework. It begins with a conceptual exploration of the nexus between land and conflict, followed by an examination of legal pluralism and competing tenure regimes. Subsequent chapters address land reform and tenure formalization, the recognition of collective and Indigenous land rights, digitalization in land administration, and rights-based and participatory governance models. Throughout these sections, interdisciplinary perspectives from law, political economy, sociology, and development studies are integrated to offer a nuanced and critical understanding of land governance and justice.

Particular attention is given to the ambivalent nature of land reforms and titling initiatives, which may reduce disputes and enhance tenure security in some contexts while simultaneously generating new tensions when they intersect with customary authority structures or exacerbate power asymmetries. Likewise, the legal recognition of community and Indigenous land rights is analyzed not only as a legal reform but as a political process that requires legitimacy, meaningful participation, and procedural fairness. The growing use of digital technologies—such as digital registries, geospatial systems, and blockchain—is examined critically, emphasizing both their potential to enhance transparency and their risks of exclusion or new forms of dispossession if implemented without inclusive governance safeguards.

This book is intended for academics, researchers, students, policymakers, legal practitioners, and civil society actors concerned with land governance, agrarian reform, natural resource management, and social justice. It is our hope that this reference work will serve both as a scholarly resource and as a platform for critical reflection, informing more just, participatory, and sustainable approaches to land-related conflict resolution.

We acknowledge that land, conflict, and justice remain dynamic and evolving fields of inquiry. Accordingly, this book does not claim to offer definitive answers. Rather, it seeks to contribute to ongoing scholarly debate and policy dialogue. Constructive feedback and critical engagement are warmly welcomed for the continued refinement of this work.

May *Land, Conflict & Justice: Governance, Power, and Pathways to Equitable Resolution* contribute meaningfully to advancing equitable land governance and strengthening pathways toward social justice.

Baubau, Februari 25, 2026
Author

Dr. Safrin Salam, S.H., M.H.

TABLE OF CONTENT

CHAPTER I

INTRODUCTION

1.1 Framing the Land–Conflict–Justice Nexus

Land is simultaneously a political arena, an economic foundation, and a symbolic anchor of identity and belonging. As a political resource, land underpins sovereignty, territorial authority, and state legitimacy. As an economic resource, it structures access to livelihoods, agricultural production, urban employment, and investment opportunities. As a symbolic resource, land embodies historical memory, cultural attachment, and collective identity. Because land operates across these dimensions at once, struggles over land rarely remain technical disputes about boundaries; they become conflicts over power, recognition, and justice.

Land governance plays a decisive role in shaping how such conflicts emerge and unfold. Governance systems structure access to resources, mobility, and urban–rural livelihood transitions, determining who can claim, defend, or transfer rights (Asaaga et al., 2020; Deininger et al., 2021; Onyebueke et al., 2020). Formalization policies, recognition of customary rights, and the degree of tenure security influence whose claims are legible to the state and whose remain vulnerable. In both rural and peri-urban contexts, insecure or contested tenure has been shown to escalate boundary disputes, forced evictions, and resource grabbing (Deininger et al., 2021; Onyebueke et al., 2020; Villiers, 2025). Where governance institutions fail to reconcile overlapping claims or provide accessible dispute resolution, latent grievances can transform into protest, violence, or prolonged litigation.

Theoretical frameworks linking tenure insecurity to conflict emphasize distributive justice, neoliberal dispossession, and legal pluralism. The concept of property rights as a "bundle" highlights how use, control, and transfer rights may be fragmented and unevenly protected, shaping incentives for cooperation or confrontation (Deininger et al., 2021). Legitimacy and legibility are equally central: when formalization enhances clarity and recognition, it may reduce uncertainty; when it privileges certain actors or disregards customary systems, it can provoke resistance (Ferree et al., 2022; Day, 2023). Political economy perspectives further illuminate how induced institutional change and institutional bricolage create uneven power asymmetries, enabling dominant actors to consolidate control while marginal groups face heightened exposure to dispossession (Asaaga et al., 2020; Onyebueke et al., 2020). In plural legal settings, overlapping statutory and customary regimes generate competing norms that can either mediate or intensify disputes (Ferree et al., 2022; Deininger et al., 2021).

Within this literature, justice is conceptualized as multidimensional. Distributive justice concerns the equitable allocation of land and compensation; procedural justice focuses on transparency, participation, and access to remedies; and spatial justice interrogates how development and dispossession are unevenly distributed across territories (Deininger et al.,

2021; Konforti, 2022; Castro, 2022; Munir, 2022). Gender equity, recognition of customary tenure, free, prior, and informed consent (FPIC), and fair compensation standards are frequently invoked benchmarks. Debates persist over whether formal law, customary institutions, or hybrid dispute resolution mechanisms are better positioned to deliver substantive justice, particularly where state institutions are weak or politicized.

Empirically, intersections among land rights, power, and violence recur across diverse contexts. Patterns of land grabbing, cattle rustling, urban dispossession, and state–corporate collaborations illustrate how conflict often emerges where power asymmetries converge with overlapping jurisdictions and competing normative orders (Khanakwa, 2022; "Legal Pluralism and Interethnic Land Conflict in the Development of the Nusantara Capital Area, East Kalimantan, Indonesia", 2026; Sulieman et al., 2024; Geyer, 2024). In such settings, land governance becomes the terrain through which authority is asserted, contested, and renegotiated. Framing the land–conflict–justice nexus therefore requires recognizing that land disputes are not isolated events but expressions of deeper institutional tensions, distributive inequalities, and struggles for recognition embedded within plural governance systems.

1.2 Scope and Objectives of the Review

This review examines the land–conflict–justice nexus with a primary focus on rural and peri-urban contexts in the Global South, while also engaging urban and post-conflict settings where land governance remains deeply contested. Over the past decade, dominant scholarship has centered on land politics, justice, and governance under conditions of legal pluralism, emphasizing how overlapping statutory and customary systems shape tenure insecurity and dispute trajectories (Wachira et al., 2023; Ayambire, 2025; Zubir & Wook, 2024; Takamura et al., 2021; Dong et al., 2022). In these contexts, land grabbing, exclusionary formalization, and contested recognition of customary and Indigenous rights have emerged as central drivers of conflict. The review therefore concentrates on settings where state-building, market expansion, and community-based tenure systems intersect, particularly across Sub-Saharan Africa, Southeast Asia, and the Pacific Islands.

Geographically, the literature is especially rich in analyses from East Africa and the Great Lakes region, Indonesia and Malaysia, and forested and frontier zones in the Pacific (Arruñada et al., 2022; Khanakwa, 2022; Badstue et al., 2020; Großmann, 2022). These regions provide illustrative cases of how plural land governance structures mediate relations between communities, investors, and state authorities. Particular attention is given to borderlands, forest frontiers, and post-conflict landscapes, where territorial control, sovereignty claims, and livelihood security converge. By foregrounding these contexts, the review captures both everyday community-level disputes and larger-scale structural conflicts tied to investment, conservation, and political transition.

Thematically, the review treats land justice as multi-dimensional and relational rather than reducible to formal titling or property registration. Contemporary scholarship links tenure security to investment incentives, gender equity, climate adaptation, and community resilience, expanding the analytical frame beyond distributive allocation to encompass procedural and recognition-based justice (Deininger et al., 2021; Hubbard, 2019; Cowan, 2025; Munshifwa et al., 2020; Nara et al., 2021). This broader conception allows the review to integrate debates on gendered access to land, Indigenous sovereignty, and intergenerational claims within climate-stressed environments. The objective is not only to map patterns of conflict but also to assess how governance reforms and justice mechanisms respond to layered social inequalities.

Methodologically, the body of literature under review is cross-disciplinary. Legal norm analysis and doctrinal studies interrogate statutory reforms and human rights incorporation; ethnographic and case study research illuminate lived experiences of tenure insecurity; GIS and remote sensing approaches trace spatial dynamics of land use and boundary disputes; and quasi-experimental designs evaluate the impacts of formalization and governance interventions (Ferree et al., 2022; Mintah et al., 2020; Misbahuddin et al., 2023; Kurnia et al., 2022; Day et al., 2020). By synthesizing these diverse methods, the review seeks to bridge normative, institutional, and empirical analyses of land-related conflict.

At the same time, important disagreements persist in the literature. Scholars debate the efficacy of legal pluralism in delivering equitable outcomes, the implementation and enforceability of free, prior, and informed consent (FPIC), and the legitimacy of customary institutions within modern constitutional orders (Tsering, 2025; Ituru et al., 2024; Istijab et al., 2022). These debates shape the guiding research questions of the review: How do plural governance systems mediate land-related conflicts? Under what conditions does tenure reform enhance or undermine justice? How do gender, identity, and sovereignty claims transform land disputes into broader struggles over recognition and authority? And which institutional arrangements most effectively translate rights into durable, conflict-sensitive governance?

By clarifying its thematic and geographic focus, and by articulating these guiding questions, the review establishes a structured foundation for examining the drivers of conflict, justice mechanisms, and governance innovations discussed in subsequent sections.

CHAPTER II

THEORETICAL AND CONCEPTUAL FOUNDATIONS

2.1 Political Economy of Land and Power

From a political economy perspective, land is a foundational source of authority, accumulation, and exclusion. Control over land structures access to surplus, shapes class formation, and underpins the material basis of state power. Land tenure regimes determine who can extract value from agricultural production, natural resources, urban development, and speculative markets. In many contexts, dispossession occurs not as an isolated event but as a systemic process embedded in investment incentives, regulatory reforms, and state–elite collusion (Ribar, 2025; Wachira et al., 2023; Kenee et al., 2020; Ferree et al., 2022). Although land titling and formalization are often justified as universalizing tenure security, empirical evidence demonstrates that outcomes are filtered through local political dynamics, customary norms, and the configuration of centralized versus decentralized governance. As a result, formalization may entrench advantages for politically connected actors while marginalizing smallholders and customary claimants.

Ownership, therefore, is not merely a legal fact but a classed and historically situated process. The notion of accumulation by dispossession captures how capitalist development pathways transform land into a vehicle for capital expansion, frequently through enclosure, commodification, and displacement (Samrin et al., 2024; Wily, 2021). Through privatization, concession agreements, and regulatory restructuring, land becomes a conduit for concentrating wealth and reorganizing social relations. Dispossession is often gradual and institutionalized, occurring through bureaucratic procedures, debt mechanisms, or development narratives that frame expropriation as modernization. In this sense, exclusion is reproduced through law and policy as much as through overt coercion.

Land control is also central to state formation and territorial consolidation. Historically and contemporarily, states mobilize land to secure taxation, attract investment, and assert sovereignty over contested spaces. Formalization initiatives, cadastral surveys, and zoning regulations enhance legibility and administrative reach, enabling governments to translate territorial claims into fiscal and political authority (Ubink & Almeida, 2023; Castro, 2022). Yet customary authorities frequently retain social legitimacy and regulatory influence, generating layered or contested sovereignty. Co-governance arrangements may emerge, but they often reflect unequal bargaining power. As states deploy land for revenue generation, infrastructure expansion, or security objectives, tensions arise between central authorities and local institutions, particularly where land is tied to identity and historical claims (Firdaus et al., 2023; Sulieman et al., 2024).

Within plural governance systems, elites often capture land institutions by navigating and instrumentalizing overlapping legal regimes. Legal pluralism can provide openings for strategic forum shopping, selective enforcement, and the co-optation of customary leaders

(Abdo, 2023; Wily, 2021). Instruments such as free, prior, and informed consent (FPIC) may be formally acknowledged yet applied in ways that legitimize pre-determined outcomes, reinforcing asymmetrical power relations (Errico & Claeys, 2020). Hybrid institutions—combining statutory authority with customary endorsement—can channel rents to political and economic elites while narrowing the space for smallholder participation (Firdaus et al., 2023). Through coercive state power, administrative discretion, and negotiated patronage, land governance becomes a mechanism for consolidating dominance rather than redistributing opportunity.

Neoliberal land reform further reconfigures these power dynamics by marketizing tenure and expanding private titles as the preferred model of security. By facilitating foreign and domestic investment, such reforms often reorder land relations in ways that privilege capital mobility over customary continuity (Gyan, 2025; Nevskaya & Kondrasheva, 2022). Processes of "green grabbing," conservation zoning, and climate-oriented land transactions can intensify dispossession under environmental justifications (Matejcek & Verne, 2022). Across rural and urban divides, these reforms reshape governance hierarchies and deepen inequalities, as access to titled property becomes a gateway to credit, compensation, and political recognition (Sesay, 2026). Seen through a political economy lens, land governance thus operates as a central terrain where authority is asserted, accumulation organized, and exclusion institutionalized within broader trajectories of capitalist development and state-building.

2.2 Legal Pluralism and Tenure Systems

Legal pluralism is a defining feature of land governance across much of the Global South, where statutory, customary, religious, and informal tenure systems coexist and interact. Rather than operating in isolation, these regimes overlap in practice, producing hybrid configurations that shape how land disputes are articulated and resolved. In many contexts, customary authorities regulate access and inheritance according to locally embedded norms, while statutory systems formalize ownership through registration, titling, and cadastral mapping. Religious courts or community-based institutions may further adjudicate family and inheritance matters, while informal market practices govern everyday transactions. This multiplicity creates both tension and opportunity. Overlapping systems often generate ambiguity in land rights, conflicting claims, and strategic bargaining among actors seeking advantage across legal forums (Ashukem, 2020; "Legal Pluralism and Interethnic Land Conflict in the Development of the Nusantara Capital Area, East Kalimantan, Indonesia", 2026; Sukirno & Wibawa, 2024; Huffel, 2024). Yet, under certain conditions, plural systems can also provide flexible pathways for negotiated settlement and participatory dispute resolution.

A central dynamic concerns the interaction between tenure formalization and customary institutions. The introduction of land certificates and registries may enhance perceived tenure security and increase land's exchange value. However, when formalization is implemented without meaningful participation or recognition of adat and other customary practices, it can erode local authority and marginalize collective claims (Honig, 2022;

Munshifwa et al., 2020). In such cases, statutory recognition may privilege individual titleholders while undermining communal governance structures. Conversely, hybrid approaches that embed customary verification processes within state registration systems tend to demonstrate stronger legitimacy and local uptake (Laine, 2026; Pfalzgraf, 2021). By incorporating community testimony, participatory mapping, or customary boundary recognition into formal procedures, these approaches reduce the gap between normative orders and mitigate the risk of overlapping or duplicate titles.

The governance implications of plural tenure regimes are significant. Hybrid systems demand inclusive and participatory planning processes, effective coordination across administrative agencies, and legal mechanisms that respect both statutory and customary authorities. Without such coordination, governance becomes plural but fragmented, reducing policy coherence and creating conditions in which some claims remain "rightless" in practice despite nominal recognition (Hubbard, 2019; Castro, 2022). Administrative overlap and unclear jurisdictional mandates can lead to certificate forgery, double titling, or contradictory court decisions, intensifying disputes rather than resolving them (Toh et al., 2023; Lin & Kaneko, 2025). In these contexts, legal pluralism becomes a terrain of competition rather than complementarity.

Synthesizing across cases, effective land governance under legal pluralism appears to rest on several conditions. First, explicit FPIC-like processes and participatory mapping can align customary boundaries with statutory registries, reducing ambiguity and strengthening legitimacy. Second, institutional bricolage that formally recognizes customary authorities within administrative and judicial mechanisms can bridge normative systems while preserving local accountability. Third, judicial and bureaucratic clarity is essential to prevent certificate duplication and strategic forum shopping. Finally, policy reforms oriented toward hybrid, rights-based regimes must balance efficiency and market integration with social justice commitments (Gyan, 2025; Sianturi & Ramli, 2025; Nasir & Saptomo, 2022; Wahid & Sulistiyono, 2025). Where these conditions are met, plural systems tend to channel disputes toward negotiated settlements and enhanced tenure security. Where they are absent, overlapping regimes amplify uncertainty, empower opportunistic actors, and entrench persistent land conflicts.

2.3 Justice Frameworks in Land Governance

Justice frameworks in land governance extend beyond the formal allocation of property titles to encompass distributive, procedural, restorative, and recognition-based dimensions. Together, these perspectives illuminate how land rights struggles are not solely about ownership, but about fairness in allocation, voice in decision-making, repair of historical harm, and affirmation of identity and collective existence. Understanding these justice dimensions is essential for analyzing how land governance either mitigates or reproduces conflict.

Distributive justice concerns the equitable allocation of benefits and burdens associated with land. In practice, distributive justice becomes visible when land titling programs, land banks, redistribution schemes, or compensation mechanisms prioritize marginalized groups and historically dispossessed communities. Yet multiple studies demonstrate that formal titling alone does not guarantee equitable outcomes. Without attention to inclusion, power asymmetries, and recognition of customary rights, titling may consolidate advantages among those already positioned to navigate bureaucratic systems (Effendi et al., 2023; Efriani et al., 2024; Pfalzgraf, 2021; Mwanza et al., 2024). Distributive gains are therefore contingent on the broader governance architecture within which land allocation occurs.

Procedural justice complements distributive concerns by focusing on the fairness, transparency, and inclusiveness of decision-making processes. Fair procedures in land recognition, free, prior, and informed consent (FPIC), participatory planning, and dispute resolution enhance the legitimacy of outcomes even where resource constraints limit redistribution. Evidence suggests that equity improves when land governance integrates customary institutions within formal administrative processes and ensures accountable intermediaries who mediate between communities and the state (Effendi et al., 2023; Großmann, 2022; Radclyffe, 2026; Mensah, 2021). Transparent consultation processes, accessible grievance mechanisms, and meaningful participation can reduce perceptions of imposed reform and help prevent escalation into conflict. In this sense, procedural justice transforms land governance from a top-down regulatory exercise into a negotiated social contract.

Recognition justice adds a further layer by emphasizing the moral and political importance of acknowledging distinct identities, histories, and normative orders. For Indigenous peoples and customary communities, recognition of land rights is foundational to self-determination and cultural survival. Without recognition, distributive and procedural reforms risk operating on a truncated understanding of entitlement. Legal pluralism, constitutional protections, and FPIC frameworks are repeatedly identified as essential instruments for embedding recognition within governance systems (M & C, 2018; Simamora, 2025; Sukirno et al., 2025; Pfalzgraf, 2021). Recognition justice reframes land disputes as struggles over sovereignty and collective dignity, not merely economic compensation. It underscores that justice requires aligning statutory law with customary tenure and territorial governance.

Restorative justice addresses situations where dispossession, displacement, or conflict has already fractured social relations. In many contexts, formal litigation is costly, slow, or ill-suited to repairing communal ties. Restorative approaches—such as Pakat Perkara deliberations, adat-based mediation, and negotiated out-of-court settlements—aim to restore rights while rebuilding trust and social harmony (Kamaruddin et al., 2023; Sukris, 2025; Matteo, 2023; Salay & Day, 2025). By integrating customary norms with restorative principles, these mechanisms can reduce cycles of retaliation and provide context-sensitive remedies. Restorative justice thus complements formal adjudication by prioritizing reconciliation and long-term stability.

Debates on social equity in land reform reveal that isolating any single justice dimension is insufficient. Reforms that focus narrowly on efficiency or market integration often reproduce or deepen inequalities, especially when they overlook gender disparities, collective rights, or historical marginalization (Naibaho & Su, 2025; Bhanye, 2025; Efriani et al., 2024; Nara et al., 2021). Inclusive land governance requires combining distributive measures with recognition of customary tenure, embedding procedural safeguards, and incorporating restorative practices where harm has occurred. Instruments such as participatory planning, land banks oriented toward marginalized groups, and gender-aware tenure reforms demonstrate how multiple justice dimensions can operate together.

By connecting distributive, procedural, restorative, and recognition-based justice, land governance frameworks reveal that land rights struggles are multidimensional. Communities contest not only who owns land, but how decisions are made, whose identities are acknowledged, and how past injustices are addressed. Integrating these justice theories provides a comprehensive lens for assessing whether governance reforms reduce conflict and advance equitable land relations, or whether they entrench exclusion under the guise of formal legality.

2.4 Political Ecology and Environmental Justice Perspectives

Political ecology provides a critical lens for understanding how ecological pressures, resource extraction, and conservation policies intersect with land-related conflicts. Rather than treating environmental degradation or scarcity as purely technical problems, political ecology situates them within unequal power relations that structure access to land and resources. Environmental conflicts often emerge where state authorities, corporations, and local communities contest land tenure, resource control, and ecological rights within layered governance systems that combine statutory, customary, and informal regimes (Nindyatmoko et al., 2022; Karambiri et al., 2020; Christensen et al., 2021). In such settings, land governance becomes the arena through which competing visions of development, conservation, and livelihood security are negotiated.

Extractive and conservation interventions frequently intensify these tensions by redistributing access to forests, minerals, water, and biodiversity. Large-scale mining, logging, plantation agriculture, and infrastructure projects often require territorial consolidation and legal reclassification of land, processes that can marginalize Indigenous and local communities (Mnwana & Bowman, 2022; Konforti, 2022; Worliczek, 2024). Similarly, conservation initiatives—whether protected areas, carbon offset schemes, or biodiversity corridors—may impose new restrictions on customary land use. Although framed as environmental protection, such measures can function as mechanisms of dispossession when they restrict mobility, exclude communities from decision-making, or fail to ensure equitable benefit-sharing (Salay & Day, 2025; Mnwana & Bowman, 2022). Political ecology thus highlights how environmental governance redistributes both ecological risks and economic opportunities.

Conservation-induced displacement raises acute justice concerns. When communities are relocated or denied access to traditional territories in the name of environmental protection, livelihoods are disrupted and cultural ties to land are weakened. These outcomes frequently violate norms of prior informed consent and undermine Indigenous territorial rights. Justice-oriented approaches emphasize recognition of collective tenure, meaningful participation in conservation planning, and FPIC-like safeguards that ensure communities are not coerced into agreements (Jackson et al., 2023; Dunkerley, 2020; Shah, 2022; Prastyadewi et al., 2021). Without these protections, conservation can replicate colonial patterns of enclosure, transforming environmental governance into a source of conflict rather than sustainability.

Extractive industries generate parallel forms of land and ecological conflict. Land grabs, forced relocations, unequal compensation, and environmental degradation often fuel local resistance and mobilize legal pluralism as communities navigate multiple forums to defend their claims (Mnwana & Bowman, 2022; Konforti, 2022; Mahanty et al., 2023; Filisi, 2025). Environmental harm—such as water contamination, deforestation, and soil degradation—can intensify perceptions of injustice, particularly where promised development benefits fail to materialize. These conflicts reveal how resource extraction is embedded in broader political economies that privilege capital accumulation over ecological stewardship and community well-being.

Links between environmental degradation and land-based violence further illustrate the intersection of ecology and conflict. Degraded habitats, shrinking agricultural land, and competition over scarce resources can provoke inter- and intra-group tensions, discrimination, and sometimes violent confrontation (Haokip, 2020; Tilley, 2020; Castro, 2022). However, the escalation of environmental stress into violence is not automatic; governance institutions and social norms mediate outcomes. Where institutions provide inclusive dispute resolution and equitable access to resources, conflicts may be contained. Where governance is fragmented or biased, environmental pressures amplify existing inequalities (Mnwana & Bowman, 2022).

The literature also underscores nuance. Some cases demonstrate institutional bricolage and negotiated compromises that align conservation goals with community rights, suggesting possibilities for hybrid governance solutions (Christensen et al., 2021; Kurnia et al., 2022). Others emphasize systemic injustice and call for structural reform, stronger recognition of customary tenure, and deeper transformations in environmental governance (Akuoko & Gerber, 2025; Yaneva-Toraman, 2024). Political ecology and environmental justice perspectives therefore enrich the land–conflict–justice nexus by revealing how ecological governance redistributes power, reshapes territorial control, and conditions the prospects for equitable and sustainable land relations.

CHAPTER III

DRIVERS AND DYNAMICS OF LAND RELATED CONFLICT

3.1 Tenure Insecurity and Competing Claims

Tenure insecurity is a central driver of land disputes because it weakens the perceived and actual protection of land claims. When individuals or communities doubt the durability of their rights, they may adopt strategic responses such as selling, subdividing, or mortgaging parcels preemptively, or seeking protection through patronage and political alliances. Such shifts can unintentionally multiply claims and complicate ownership histories (Elliott, 2021; Munshifwa et al., 2020; Deininger et al., 2021; Tirivangasi et al., 2023). In contexts where tenure remains unsettled, opportunistic actors may exploit ambiguity to transfer land informally or secure documentation through selective bureaucratic access. Rather than stabilizing property relations, insecurity produces a cascade of competing transactions that heighten the likelihood of dispute.

Beyond individual transactions, tenure insecurity fuels broader patterns of social and spatial inequality. Groups with limited access to formal documentation, political representation, or financial resources often find their claims more vulnerable to contestation. Overlapping systems—customary, statutory, and informal—can reinforce these inequalities by recognizing some rights while marginalizing others. As a result, insecurity becomes embedded in plural governance structures, reproducing contested claims across generations and territories (Elliott, 2021; Claessens et al., 2021; Akuoko & Gerber, 2025). Where tenure insecurity intersects with poverty or marginalization, disputes may escalate into more entrenched conflicts over recognition and survival.

Overlapping land claims in plural legal systems are frequently rooted in the coexistence—and occasional conflict—between customary and statutory rights. Customary authorities may allocate land according to lineage, community membership, or negotiated consent, while statutory regimes prioritize formal registration and cadastral demarcation. In addition, multiple adat traditions or religious norms may coexist within a single territory, generating divergent inheritance and allocation rules. Dual governance arrangements in land administration further complicate matters when local and central authorities operate parallel systems without clear coordination (Claessens et al., 2021; Tirivangasi et al., 2023; Iswanto et al., 2022; Geyer, 2024). Rapid urbanization, infrastructure expansion, or resource-driven expropriation can outpace mapping and registration processes, intensifying competition for land and multiplying overlapping claims.

Cadastral weaknesses compound these tensions. In many contexts, historical boundaries are poorly documented, survey records are fragmented across agencies, and land mutations or transfers are not promptly updated in registries. Delays in registration create windows during which multiple actors may claim the same parcel. Even digital or blockchain-based registries, while promising greater transparency, may fail to capture customary tenure arrangements or communal boundaries if not designed inclusively (Joshi, 2021; Mintah et al., 2020; Akuoko & Gerber, 2025). The resulting discrepancies between on-the-ground realities and official records generate disputes over boundaries, inheritance, and ownership validity. Where administrative capacity is weak, these technical shortcomings can become flashpoints for confrontation.

Elite capture further intensifies tenure-related disputes. Politically connected actors may leverage bureaucratic discretion, legal pluralism, or patronage networks to secure documentation that overrides customary claims. Insecure tenure creates opportunities for selective enforcement and strategic titling, enabling elites to consolidate landholdings at the expense of smallholders. This dynamic often remains opaque until contested through protest or litigation. Evidence links unclear land rights and administrative lacunae to episodes of violence, forced displacement, and mass mobilization, particularly where state authorities or investors assert claims without adequate consultation or consent (Deininger et al., 2021; Wily, 2021; Akuoko & Gerber, 2025). In such cases, disputes are not solely about boundaries but about legitimacy, accountability, and the distribution of power.

Taken together, unclear boundaries, weak documentation, elite capture, and overlapping claims create a volatile terrain in which tenure insecurity becomes both cause and consequence of land conflict. Disputes persist where governance systems fail to reconcile plural norms, update registries effectively, and protect vulnerable claimants. Addressing tenure insecurity therefore requires not only technical cadastral reform but also institutional coordination, inclusive recognition of customary rights, and safeguards against opportunistic appropriation. Without these measures, competing claims will continue to undermine stability and fuel recurring land-based conflict.

3.2 Large Scale Land Acquisitions and Displacement

Large scale land acquisitions (LSLAs) have emerged as a prominent driver of land-related conflict across agribusiness, mining, infrastructure, and conservation sectors. These acquisitions frequently entail enclosure of customary lands, reclassification of communal territories, and transfer of control to private or state-backed investors. Social conflicts arise where state–private investment incentives collide with locally embedded tenure norms, producing disputes over legitimacy, consent, and resource access (Chilombo & Horst, 2021; Christensen et al., 2021). Evidence from African contexts, including Liberia, demonstrates that legibility gaps between formal concession agreements and customary occupation intensify displacement pressures, triggering protests and contested concessions (Christensen et al., 2021; Afrizal & Berenschot, 2022). Where mapping, consultation, and compensation processes are opaque or exclusionary, land acquisitions become flashpoints for broader grievances against governance institutions.

Agribusiness and mining investments often erode or redefine community land rights by granting concession power to corporate actors who operate through statutory authorization while bypassing customary claims. Legal pluralism and unclear tenure arrangements weaken security, as communities struggle to assert collective rights within formal administrative systems (Christensen et al., 2021; Tripathi et al., 2025; Geyer, 2024; Arruñada et al., 2022). Disputes commonly center on compensation adequacy, the authenticity of consent, and the distribution of project benefits. Debates surrounding free, prior, and informed consent (FPIC) and collective tenure recognition recur as potential safeguards, yet implementation remains uneven and contested (Afrizal et al., 2022; Deininger et al., 2021; Nara et al., 2021). In many instances, procedural shortcomings undermine distributive outcomes, deepening mistrust between communities, investors, and the state.

Patterns of resistance reflect the plural normative terrain in which these conflicts unfold. Communities mobilize rights-based strategies such as civil protests, strategic litigation, and appeals to constitutional or human rights standards. Simultaneously, customary-based discourses frame claims in terms of ancestral territory and moral legitimacy. Counter-mapping initiatives, ad hoc mediation efforts, and community coalitions seek recognition within hybrid legal orders (Afrizal & Berenschot, 2022; Afrizal et al., 2022; Cai, 2022; Ayambire, 2025). Transnational advocacy networks and international norms have, in some contexts, reshaped policy debates and constrained investor practices, as illustrated in FPIC-related reforms in Indonesia and broader African land governance discussions (Matteo, 2023; Valencia, 2021). These dynamics demonstrate that resistance is not merely reactive but embedded in evolving governance frameworks.

Displacement constitutes one of the most severe consequences of LSLAs. Loss of access to farmland, forests, grazing areas, or fisheries undermines livelihoods, erodes household assets, and exacerbates food insecurity. Where compensation fails to reflect long-term economic and cultural losses, affected populations face heightened vulnerability and social fragmentation (Nkansah-Dwamena, 2021; Noufé, 2023). The transfer of land control to capital-intensive enterprises often disrupts local economic systems, reinforcing dependency and inequality. These impacts fuel demands for land restoration, reform of compensation regimes, and participatory governance arrangements that include affected communities in decision-making (Nara et al., 2021; Bahmid et al., 2024).

Conflicts linked to large-scale land acquisitions thus reveal the intersection of political economy, legal pluralism, and justice claims. Where governance systems prioritize investment efficiency over recognition of customary rights and meaningful participation, enclosure and displacement generate sustained contestation. Conversely, contexts that institutionalize FPIC-like safeguards, transparent compensation frameworks, and inclusive negotiation mechanisms show greater potential for mitigating conflict. LSLAs therefore represent not only economic transactions but arenas in which authority, legitimacy, and social justice are actively renegotiated.

3.3 Climate Change, Environmental Stress, and Resource Competition

Climate change intensifies land pressures and conflict risks by amplifying environmental stressors such as drought, rainfall variability, flooding, and ecosystem degradation. These pressures tighten competition over scarce land, water, and ecosystem services, particularly in agrarian and pastoral regions where livelihoods depend directly on natural resources (Zikargie, 2025; Hosen et al., 2020; Effendi et al., 2023). As environmental conditions deteriorate, the carrying capacity of land declines, agricultural yields fluctuate, and grazing areas shrink, generating new disputes over access and control. In contexts where governance institutions are already fragile, ecological shocks can expose and deepen existing tenure ambiguities.

Multiple studies link drought and climate stress to increased land clashes, migration flows, and heightened vulnerability in regions characterized by weak tenure security (Arficho & Thiel, 2020; Hosen et al., 2020; Afrizal & Berenschot, 2022). Drought-induced yield declines and pasture scarcity often push communities to expand cultivation into contested territories or migrate toward peri-urban zones, intensifying competition for land and water rights. Where tenure systems are informal or divided between customary and statutory regimes, climate variability exacerbates overlapping claims and administrative confusion (Arficho & Thiel, 2020; Effendi et al., 2023; Afrizal & Berenschot, 2022). Environmental stress thus acts as a catalyst, accelerating disputes that are rooted in structural governance weaknesses.

Evidence further suggests that eviction risks and contested access to land increase when climate variability intersects with insecure tenure arrangements. As land values fluctuate due to shifting resource productivity, politically connected actors may seek to consolidate control over areas perceived as strategically valuable, particularly where new irrigation, infrastructure, or adaptation investments are planned. In plural legal systems, ambiguity regarding water rights, communal grazing areas, or forest access intensifies friction among groups (Hosen et al., 2020; Effendi et al., 2023). Climate stress therefore not only reduces resource availability but also reshapes incentive structures for appropriation and exclusion.

Adaptation policies play a critical mediating role in shaping whether climate impacts escalate or mitigate conflict. Policies that strengthen recognition of customary rights, formalize tenure inclusively, promote co-management arrangements, and embed FPIC-like safeguards can enhance tenure security and build resilience (Claessens et al., 2021; Honig, 2022; Ferree et al., 2022). By integrating participatory processes and acknowledging plural legal orders, such measures reduce uncertainty and foster cooperation over scarce resources. Conversely, adaptation strategies that centralize authority, reclassify land under new risk regimes, or prioritize large-scale investments without community consent may reinforce state-led dispossession and intensify grievances (Schreiner & Koppen, 2020). In these cases, climate governance becomes an additional layer of contestation within already fragmented institutional landscapes.

Debates persist regarding whether scarcity itself or governance failure is the primary driver of climate-related land conflict. While ecological stress undeniably increases pressure on limited resources, evidence indicates that scarcity under weak, fragmented governance—

characterized by overlapping authorities and limited dispute resolution capacity—more reliably precipitates conflict than scarcity alone (Claessens et al., 2021; Ferree et al., 2022; Matteo, 2023). Effective governance reforms, including transparent allocation mechanisms and inclusive institutions, can mitigate climate-induced disputes even amid environmental constraints (Effendi et al., 2023).

In sum, climate change intensifies land pressures by amplifying resource scarcity, altering livelihood strategies, and exposing tenure vulnerabilities. However, the translation of environmental stress into conflict is mediated by governance quality, recognition of customary rights, and the inclusiveness of adaptation policies. Climate-related land conflicts thus reveal the intertwined nature of ecological transformation and institutional resilience within the broader land–conflict–justice nexus.

3.4 Urbanization, Informality, and Peri-Urban Expansion

Rapid urban expansion has become one of the most significant contemporary drivers of land conflict, particularly in peri-urban zones and informal settlements where demographic growth and spatial transformation outpace regulatory capacity. As cities extend into surrounding rural territories, competition intensifies among households, customary authorities, private developers, and state institutions. Peri-urban and slum areas frequently expand into increasingly scarce land, provoking competing claims and overlapping jurisdictions (López, 2025; "Legal Pluralism and Interethnic Land Conflict in the Development of the Nusantara Capital Area, East Kalimantan, Indonesia", 2026; Geyer, 2024). Rising land values linked to infrastructure projects, new capitals, industrial zones, and speculative real estate markets further incentivize contestation. In such settings, urban growth is not merely a demographic process but a reconfiguration of authority, tenure, and legitimacy.

Peri-urban land transitions are especially prone to dispute because they generate ambiguity across customary, state, and private tenure regimes. Customary leaders may continue allocating land according to lineage-based or communal norms, even as statutory authorities introduce formal registration systems and private firms secure development concessions. This coexistence produces overlapping titles, double allocations, and fragmented records that intensify uncertainty (Ferree et al., 2022; Munshifwa et al., 2020; Onyebueke et al., 2020). Governance becomes plural but not necessarily coordinated, and residents may struggle to determine which institution has ultimate jurisdiction. As land shifts from agricultural or customary use toward commercial and residential functions, disputes emerge not only over boundaries but over the legitimacy of different normative orders (Geyer, 2024). Where governance mechanisms fail to remain legible and inclusive to residents, peri-urban expansion becomes a persistent source of conflict.

Eviction and regularization policies illustrate the justice dilemmas embedded in urban land governance. State-led redevelopment and infrastructure initiatives often require land consolidation, rezoning, or expropriation, disproportionately affecting residents of informal settlements. Evictions carried out without adequate consultation, compensation, or relocation support undermine tenure security and intensify claims grounded in housing rights and social equity (Day et al., 2020; Geyer, 2024). Conversely, regularization programs can legitimize informal claims, improve service provision, and reduce uncertainty. However, if regularization criteria privilege those with documentation or exclude renters, migrants, and women-headed households, reforms may reproduce discrimination and deepen vulnerability (Bhanye, 2025). The justice implications of urban reform therefore depend on how distributive and procedural safeguards are embedded in policy design.

Informal settlements demonstrate how residents actively negotiate land rights within plural legal environments. Rather than existing outside governance, informal neighborhoods often operate through layered arrangements that combine customary recognition, informal sale agreements, neighborhood attestations, and strategic engagement with local officials. Such practices generate forms of de facto tenure security, even if not formally recognized by cadastral systems (Ferree et al., 2022; Asaaga et al., 2020). Residents frequently leverage social networks, local institutions, and political intermediaries to secure incremental recognition, especially during periods of electoral mobilization or urban planning reform ("Legal Pluralism and Interethnic Land Conflict in the Development of the Nusantara Capital Area, East Kalimantan, Indonesia", 2026; Zaim et al., 2020). These negotiations reveal that informality is not synonymous with illegality but represents an adaptive response to exclusionary or inaccessible formal systems.

Debates persist regarding whether formal titling improves or jeopardizes long-term tenure security in informal settlements. On one hand, titles may reduce eviction risk, facilitate access to credit, and enhance property value. On the other hand, market integration can trigger gentrification pressures and speculative acquisition, displacing lower-income residents. In rapidly growing cities, the conversion of informal neighborhoods into formal property markets can intensify inequalities if safeguards are absent. Urban land conflicts thus reflect tensions between market-driven development and social protection, particularly where governance institutions lack capacity to regulate speculative behavior (Geyer, 2024).

Overall, the literature suggests that a pluralist governance approach is necessary to advance justice in rapidly urbanizing contexts. Combining recognition of customary authority, participatory urban planning, and targeted, equity-oriented formalization can reduce ambiguity and strengthen legitimacy (Ferree et al., 2022; Geyer, 2024; Onyebueke et al., 2020; Boamah & Amoako, 2019). Participatory planning processes that include peri-urban residents, transparent coordination among agencies, and accessible dispute resolution mechanisms enhance procedural justice and mitigate escalation. Without such integrative approaches, urban expansion risks entrenching elite capture, fragmenting tenure systems, and perpetuating cycles of eviction and protest.

Urbanization, informality, and peri-urban expansion therefore reveal how land conflicts are embedded in broader transformations of territory and governance. Rapid spatial growth reorders property relations, reshapes power hierarchies, and tests the capacity of institutions to reconcile competing claims. Where governance frameworks remain exclusionary or opaque, urban land transitions intensify conflict. Where they integrate plural tenure systems with participatory and rights-based safeguards, cities may become arenas not only of expansion but of negotiated and more equitable land governance.

CHAPTER IV

CONFLICT TYPOLOGIES AND ACTORS

4.1 Localized Community Level Disputes

Localized community-level land disputes represent one of the most pervasive yet underexamined dimensions of the land–conflict–justice nexus. Unlike large-scale acquisitions or state-led expropriation, these conflicts unfold within and between households, kinship groups, and neighboring communities. They frequently concern inheritance, boundary demarcation, and the authority of customary leaders, and are shaped by demographic pressures, legal pluralism, and shifting governance arrangements. Population growth, land scarcity, and expanding claims by state institutions, private investors, or infrastructure projects intensify competition at the local level, transforming everyday disagreements into protracted disputes (Nuryasinta & Wardoyo, 2024; Sukirno & Wibawa, 2024; Sarfo et al., 2024). As arable land fragments and values rise, intra-community tensions become more visible and politically charged.

Inheritance systems play a particularly significant role in structuring these disputes. Divergent expectations regarding succession, lineage entitlements, and gendered rights often generate conflict among siblings, extended family members, or clan groups. In some contexts, postponement of formal division—where heirs continue joint use without clear demarcation—creates ambiguity that later escalates into disagreement when land is sold or mortgaged. Unequal bequest practices, ritualized allocation ceremonies, or interpretations of religious inheritance norms may further complicate claims (Munir, 2022; Harris & Honig, 2023; Effendi et al., 2023). These inheritance-related tensions are not merely technical matters of distribution; they reflect deeper questions of legitimacy, recognition, and social obligation within customary systems.

Boundary disputes similarly emerge where historical markers—trees, rivers, stones, or oral testimony—are contested or have disappeared due to environmental change or development. As land scarcity increases, previously flexible boundaries may become rigidly defended. The entry of external actors, such as infrastructure agencies or private developers, can sharpen these disputes by introducing new valuation standards and documentation requirements. In plural legal environments, differences between customary demarcation and statutory cadastral maps may generate overlapping claims that reverberate within communities. Thus, inter-household conflicts are often embedded within broader processes of legal pluralism and administrative reform (Sukirno & Wibawa, 2024).

Customary leaders and mediation institutions play central roles in processing and resolving localized land disputes. Mechanisms such as Pakat Perkara, Kalosara, and customary courts blend local wisdom with Islamic principles or elements of state law, reflecting adaptive forms of institutional bricolage (Seko & Soa, 2025; Ramli et al., 2024; Kamaruddin et al., 2023; Sukris, 2025). These institutions often prioritize dialogue, reconciliation, and restoration of social harmony over adversarial adjudication. Their legitimacy derives from proximity to disputants, familiarity with lineage histories, and alignment with community norms. However, their authority can be contested when formal courts assert jurisdiction or when external actors question the impartiality of customary leaders. Tensions between customary and statutory forums may create parallel proceedings, prolonging disputes rather than resolving them.

Social norms and locally embedded concepts of justice significantly shape how disputes are understood and settled. Restorative and consensual approaches emphasize repairing relationships, reaffirming communal bonds, and achieving outcomes perceived as socially legitimate rather than strictly legalistic. Restorative-adat principles guide mediation through collective deliberation, apology, compensation, and ritual affirmation (Sukriono et al., 2025; Sukirno & Wibawa, 2024; Sukris, 2025). These norms can foster durable settlements by aligning resolution with shared moral frameworks. At the same time, they may diverge from formal legal procedures that prioritize documentary evidence and statutory rights, creating friction where outcomes are challenged in state courts (Berenschot & Saraswati, 2024). Such divergences underscore the complexity of justice within plural governance systems.

Localized disputes therefore cannot be reduced to isolated quarrels; they are shaped by intersecting demographic, legal, and political pressures. Land scarcity amplifies competition, inheritance norms structure expectations, and plural governance frameworks provide multiple arenas for claim-making. Effective resolution requires integrating customary leadership with accessible alternative dispute resolution mechanisms and ensuring that outcomes are legible within broader legal systems. Where customary and formal institutions collaborate transparently and respect community norms, disputes are more likely to culminate in negotiated and socially accepted settlements. Where authority is fragmented or politicized, localized conflicts risk escalating into wider social divisions.

In sum, inter-household and intra-community land disputes illuminate how the land–conflict–justice nexus operates at the most immediate social scale. They reveal the centrality of inheritance, boundary clarity, and customary authority in shaping everyday experiences of tenure security. Addressing these disputes demands governance frameworks that respect legal pluralism, strengthen mediation capacity, and harmonize restorative community practices with statutory safeguards. Only through such integrative approaches can localized conflicts be transformed from sources of fragmentation into opportunities for reaffirming equitable and legitimate land governance.

4.2 Identity-Based and Ethno-Political Land Conflicts

Land frequently functions as a central axis of ethnic mobilization and politicized identity, transforming territorial claims into broader struggles over belonging, sovereignty, and exclusion. In many contexts, ethnic groups articulate claims to land not merely as economic entitlements but as expressions of historical presence, ancestral authority, and moral ownership. Territory becomes a symbolic and material anchor through which communities assert collective rights and demarcate insiders from outsiders (Arruñada et al., 2022; Afrizal & Berenschot, 2022; Berenschot & Saraswati, 2024). When state boundaries, administrative zoning, or development concessions intersect with these deeply embedded territorial imaginaries, land disputes can escalate into identity-based confrontation.

Territorial claims often operate as proxies for national or nativist projects. Competing groups may frame land as the basis of authentic citizenship, cultural survival, or indigenous sovereignty, positioning rival claimants as encroachers or beneficiaries of unjust state favoritism. Such narratives gain traction where formal demarcations collide with existing livelihoods and customary land use patterns (Zigashane, 2025; Matteo, 2023; Deininger et al., 2021). In rapidly transforming regions—such as new capital developments, mining frontiers, or agrarian expansion zones—these tensions are amplified as land becomes both economically valuable and symbolically charged. Violence may erupt when ethnicized territorial claims intersect with resource scarcity, political competition, and weak dispute resolution mechanisms.

Historical land grievances are central to understanding the intensity of identity-based conflicts. Colonial and postcolonial regimes frequently reconfigured land tenure through unequal titling systems, expropriation for plantations or extractive industries, and centralization of authority over customary territories. These legacies persist as collective memories of dispossession, shaping contemporary mobilization (Hubbard, 2019; Mnwana & Bowman, 2022; Toh et al., 2023; Vunibola & Scheyvens, 2023; Arficho & Thiel, 2020). Where state-led development or conservation initiatives have undermined customary rights, grievances accumulate across generations. Land disputes thus become vehicles for redressing perceived historical injustice rather than isolated contemporary disagreements.

Conflicts intensify when customary tenure is marginalized by formal legal regimes or when migrant and investor claims collide with autochthonous conceptions of ownership. In plural legal systems, state recognition of formal titles may delegitimize long-standing customary claims, particularly when documentation requirements exclude oral histories or communal tenure forms (Fuad et al., 2023; Mahanty et al., 2023; Mintah et al., 2020). Migrant populations, often encouraged by state settlement schemes or economic opportunity, may acquire land through statutory mechanisms that appear lawful but clash with local notions of territorial entitlement. Such collisions can foster narratives of invasion or demographic threat, reinforcing ethnic polarization and deepening mistrust between communities.

Nationalism further intertwines with land rights by invoking territory as the foundation of sovereignty and statehood. Governments may mobilize land formalization to assert centralized authority, standardize tenure, or attract investment, framing these initiatives as instruments of national development. Yet formalization can either empower communities—

by clarifying rights and enhancing recognition—or displace them when reforms disregard plural legal frameworks (Ferree et al., 2022; Uma, 2023; Nkansah-Dwamena, 2021; Hosen et al., 2020). Where plural systems are harmonized and participatory safeguards embedded, formalization may reduce uncertainty. Where they clash, titling can entrench exclusion and exacerbate identity-based tensions.

In post-colonial identity struggles, land frequently becomes a marker of indigeneity and collective memory. Revived claims to ulayat or customary territories reflect efforts to reclaim autonomy and reassert cultural continuity. These movements often draw upon narratives of ancestral stewardship and resistance to external domination, framing land restitution as both material recovery and symbolic restoration (Sukirno & Wibawa, 2024; Uma, 2023; Onyebueke et al., 2020; Akhtar, 2023). Legal pluralism and hybrid dispute mechanisms have emerged in some contexts as pragmatic responses to these tensions, seeking to restore legitimacy by integrating customary authority with formal legal recognition. Such arrangements, however, remain contested where state institutions fear fragmentation of sovereignty or loss of regulatory control.

Identity-based land conflicts thus operate at the intersection of memory, law, and political mobilization. They are intensified by historical dispossession, uneven development, migration, and governance fragmentation. While land may appear as the immediate object of dispute, underlying struggles concern recognition, citizenship, and the distribution of authority. Effective mitigation requires acknowledging historical grievances, embedding plural legal recognition, and ensuring that development or formalization initiatives do not erase culturally embedded tenure systems. Without such integrative approaches, territorial disputes risk hardening into enduring ethno-political divisions that extend beyond land governance into broader arenas of state legitimacy and social cohesion.

4.3 State–Citizen and Corporate–Community Conflicts

Conflicts between states, corporate actors, and local communities frequently arise in the context of land reform, expropriation, and large-scale private investment. These disputes are typically triggered when communities face displacement, inadequate or opaque compensation, and weak consultation processes, particularly where customary land rights are ignored or devalued. Empirical evidence documents recurrent protests and rights-based resistance in contexts where free, prior, and informed consent (FPIC), fair compensation, and meaningful participation are absent or only nominally implemented (Krismantoro, 2025; Errico & Claeys, 2020; Berenschot & Saraswati, 2024; Geyer, 2024; Fuad et al., 2023). In such cases, expropriation is perceived not as lawful public purpose action but as dispossession that privileges state or corporate interests over community rights.

Nuanced patterns of resistance reveal how legitimacy is contested in these encounters. In Indonesia and other plural legal settings, communities sometimes mobilize what has been described as "rightless" discourse, foregrounding customary norms and moral claims over formal statutory entitlements when engaging in protest (Berenschot & Saraswati, 2024). Counter-mapping initiatives and face-off dynamics at expropriation frontiers demonstrate how competing narratives of legality and legitimacy unfold in practice, as communities seek to make their territorial claims visible against official cadastral maps (Tilley, 2020; Cai, 2022). These strategies underscore that state–citizen conflict is not solely about compensation levels but about recognition, authority, and the credibility of governance processes.

Governance failures frequently exacerbate corporate–community disputes. Lack of coherent multi-actor governance, overlapping statutory and customary regimes, and weak participation of local stakeholders create institutional vacuums in which grievances accumulate. Opaque valuation methods, non-inclusive spatial planning, and the absence of effective dispute resolution institutions undermine trust and accountability (Gwaleba et al., 2023; Geyer, 2024; Maring, 2022; Mawere et al., 2021). Dual legal systems and legitimacy gaps further complicate enforcement, enabling strategic forum shopping by powerful actors while marginalizing communities. In response, collective action and hybrid dispute mechanisms often emerge as communities attempt to navigate fragmented governance landscapes (Boamah & Amoako, 2019; Takamura et al., 2021; Cai, 2022). Such hybridity reflects both institutional weakness and adaptive negotiation.

State-backed investment projects reshape local land relations by accelerating enclosure and commodification. Collaboration between governments and corporate entities often reconfigures tenure systems, reallocates resource access, and transforms livelihoods. Research on land grabbing and extractive-sector expansion shows clustering of conflict around expropriation processes and negotiations conducted under plural legal orders (Arruñada et al., 2022; Afrizal & Berenschot, 2022; Gupta, 2021; Iswanto et al., 2022; Kurnia et al., 2022). These investments frequently intensify legitimacy struggles between customary claimants and investors, particularly where benefit-sharing arrangements are unclear or inequitable. Without safeguards such as FPIC and transparent revenue distribution, development narratives may mask redistributive inequities.

Addressing land-related human rights violations requires robust accountability mechanisms. FPIC requirements, judicial review processes, and alignment with international rights frameworks such as UNDRIP and UNDROP provide normative anchors for evaluating state and corporate conduct (Errico & Claeys, 2020). Independent oversight bodies, transparent land registries, and procedural reforms that enhance access to courts and administrative remedies can strengthen institutional credibility (Geyer, 2024; Maring, 2022; Debsu, 2024). Integrating customary governance with formal adjudication systems may also enhance accountability by grounding decisions in locally legitimate norms.

Debates persist regarding whether governance hybridity should be minimized or explicitly designed. Some scholars argue that institutional hybridity and agonistic planning are inevitable features of plural legal environments and should be structured through clear accountability frameworks rather than suppressed (Ayambire, 2025; Gwaleba et al., 2023). Designing institutions that manage contestation transparently may reduce escalation and transform adversarial state–citizen relations into negotiated governance processes. Ultimately, state–citizen and corporate–community land conflicts illuminate how authority, legality, and justice are continuously contested within development and reform trajectories.

Effective resolution depends on embedding participation, transparency, and plural recognition within land governance systems.

4.4 Gendered Dimensions of Land Conflict

Gender inequality profoundly shapes the dynamics and outcomes of land-related conflicts. Women frequently experience reduced tenure security, limited access to formal justice mechanisms, and weaker bargaining positions within households and communities. These asymmetries influence how disputes are framed, adjudicated, and resolved, often resulting in poorer outcomes for women when land rights are contested (Sesay, 2026; Ubink & Almeida, 2023; Kansanga et al., 2020; Deininger et al., 2021). Gendered power hierarchies intersect with legal pluralism, customary norms, and economic vulnerability, producing patterns of exclusion that are embedded in both formal and informal land governance systems.

Women's land rights disputes often arise within households, particularly in cases of inheritance, divorce, widowhood, or marital dissolution. In contexts where land is transmitted patrilineally or where male household heads are formally recognized as primary titleholders, women's claims may be treated as secondary or derivative. This structural positioning weakens their negotiating power when disputes emerge. Even where statutory law formally recognizes gender equality, implementation gaps and social norms can undermine practical enforcement (Ubink & Almeida, 2023; Deininger et al., 2021). Consequently, intra-household inequality is not merely a private matter but a core component of the broader land–conflict–justice nexus.

Barriers to women's access to formal land justice are significant and multifaceted. Legal pluralism can privilege male-dominated customary authorities or religious courts that interpret inheritance and marital property rules in ways that disadvantage women (Bartolomei, 2025; Ubink & Almeida, 2023). Formal judicial systems, meanwhile, may be geographically distant, procedurally complex, and financially inaccessible. Delays, evidentiary burdens, and biased adjudication practices further erode women's confidence in legal remedies (Singh & Bhatnagar, 2024; Khanakwa, 2022). In such environments, women may refrain from pursuing claims altogether, relying instead on informal negotiation even when outcomes are inequitable. The result is a cycle in which gender-based exclusion becomes normalized within dispute resolution processes.

Inheritance laws and practices constitute a central arena of gendered land conflict. In many contexts, male heirs are privileged in succession systems, while daughters' rights are curtailed through dowry arrangements, marital relocation norms, or cultural expectations of land transfer through male lineage. These arrangements produce ongoing disputes over bequest and usufruct rights, particularly when economic pressures heighten the value of land (Singh & Bhatnagar, 2024; Genicot & Hernandez-de-Benito, 2022; Gwaleba et al., 2023; Yiran et al., 2025). Widows may face eviction from marital land upon the death of a spouse, and divorced women may struggle to claim shares in jointly cultivated property. Such disputes illustrate how gendered norms intersect with economic vulnerability, reinforcing patterns of dispossession.

Land formalization and titling reforms present both opportunities and risks for women's tenure security. When designed with gender-sensitive safeguards—such as joint titling provisions, explicit recognition of women's rights under customary law, accessible adjudication processes, and FPIC-related protections—formalization can strengthen women's claims and enhance bargaining power (Deininger et al., 2021; Ubink & Almeida, 2023). Evidence suggests that recognition of women as independent rights holders improves investment incentives and household welfare outcomes. However, formalization can also produce unintended consequences. If reforms prioritize individual ownership models that disregard secondary or use rights traditionally held by women, titling may erode the very claims it seeks to secure (Sesay, 2026; Fuad et al., 2023). In market-oriented reform contexts, neoliberal pressures may further marginalize women by consolidating land in the hands of male elites or external investors.

Gender-based exclusion in land governance is not confined to household-level dynamics; it also shapes participation in community decision-making and collective negotiations with state or corporate actors. Women are often underrepresented in customary councils, land committees, and consultation forums, limiting their influence over allocation and compensation processes (Kansanga et al., 2020). Where women's voices are absent from participatory mechanisms, governance reforms risk reproducing existing inequalities. Addressing this imbalance requires procedural reforms that institutionalize gender-responsive participation and ensure accountability in both customary and formal institutions.

Equitable land governance therefore demands an integrated approach that combines gender-responsive tenure protections, reform of discriminatory inheritance rules, and alignment between formal institutions and customary practices. Policy frameworks that explicitly incorporate gender equality provisions, capacity-building initiatives for women's legal literacy, and accessible dispute resolution mechanisms can enhance women's tenure security and dispute outcomes (Deininger et al., 2021; Ituru et al., 2024; Gwaleba et al., 2023). Aligning statutory reforms with culturally legitimate yet non-discriminatory customary norms is particularly critical in plural legal contexts.

In sum, gendered dimensions of land conflict reveal how structural inequality permeates both the origins and resolution of disputes. Women's land rights struggles are shaped by inheritance systems, legal pluralism, and market-driven reforms that can either empower or dispossess. Without deliberate gender-responsive governance design, land reforms may inadvertently entrench disparities. Embedding equality, participation, and recognition within land governance institutions is therefore essential not only for protecting women's rights but also for advancing broader objectives of justice and conflict mitigation.

CHAPTER V

JUSTICE MECHANISMS AND DISPUTE RESOLUTION PATHWAYS

5.1 Customary and Informal Dispute Resolution

Customary and informal dispute resolution mechanisms occupy a central place in the governance of land conflicts, particularly in rural and peri-urban settings characterized by strong kinship ties and plural legal systems. Traditional authorities, mediation practices, and community-based justice forums often function as first-instance institutions for resolving disputes over inheritance, boundaries, and access rights. Their effectiveness derives from cultural resonance, proximity to disputants, and the capacity to embed resolution within shared moral frameworks. Empirical evidence suggests that customary institutions can deliver faster and contextually legitimate outcomes, particularly where mediation prioritizes social harmonization over adversarial adjudication (Kamaruddin et al., 2023; Sukirno & Wibawa, 2024; Ramli et al., 2024; Iswari et al., 2025). In settings such as Aceh or Kalosara-type practices, mediation processes yield settlements aligned with local norms and collective understandings of justice, reinforcing social order and minimizing escalation (Kamaruddin et al., 2023; Ramli et al., 2024).

The strengths of customary mechanisms are closely tied to their restorative orientation. Rather than emphasizing punitive sanctions, these systems often privilege dialogue, consensus-building, apology, and compensation structured around adat or Islam-informed principles. Outcomes are legitimized not primarily through written documentation but through collective acknowledgment and ritual affirmation. In contexts where disputants share longstanding social ties, this approach can reduce litigation costs, preserve relationships, and prevent conflict from spreading across kin networks (Sukirno & Wibawa, 2024). However, effectiveness is not uniform. Where state interests prevail, land values rise sharply, or market pressures intensify, customary mechanisms may be sidelined or struggle to enforce agreements. In such circumstances, formal courts or hybrid ADR arrangements may outperform customary forums in terms of consistency and enforceability (Wahid & Sulistiyono, 2025; Sulaiman & Satriawan, 2021). Broader analyses indicate that customary mechanisms function best where they are informally empowered and socially embedded, and may underperform where statutory adjudication or commodified land markets dominate (Sukirno & Wibawa, 2024; Sulaiman & Satriawan, 2021; Deininger et al., 2021; Sumarni et al., 2023).

Legitimacy remains a central challenge for traditional land authorities. Overlapping jurisdictions between adat leaders, state courts, and religious institutions can generate confusion and erode trust in dispute outcomes. Lack of transparent land data, unclear boundary records, and competing claims of authority weaken enforcement capacity and foster perceptions of injustice (Ramli et al., 2024; Sulaiman & Satriawan, 2021; Deininger et al., 2021; Toumbourou & Dressler, 2020). In plural systems where state, Islamic, and customary norms intersect, disputants may strategically navigate multiple forums, undermining the finality of decisions. Some scholars advocate for formal recognition and institutional embedding of customary courts within plural governance frameworks to enhance coherence and authority (Sukirno & Wibawa, 2024). Others caution that excessive formalization risks displacing local legitimacy if processes become bureaucratized or detached from participatory norms (Sulaiman & Satriawan, 2021; Deininger et al., 2021; Geyer, 2024). Nuanced evidence suggests that legitimacy improves when local actors participate actively in land data collection, participatory mapping, and dispute processes that bridge adat and state law (Nuryasinta & Wardoyo, 2024; Sulaiman & Satriawan, 2021).

Informal mediation also offers pathways for addressing power asymmetries embedded in land disputes. Face-to-face negotiation settings can humanize conflicts and allow mediators to balance interests through socially recognized authority rather than coercive sanctions. Restorative justice principles embedded in community forums may enable marginalized parties to voice grievances in culturally familiar settings (Sukriono et al., 2025; Nuryasinta & Wardoyo, 2024; Sukris, 2025). By relying on village leaders, elders, or kin-based intermediaries, mediation can recalibrate disputes that might otherwise escalate in formal adversarial settings (Deininger et al., 2021). Hybrid ADR arrangements—where customary mediation is complemented by formal oversight—have been associated with strengthened social cohesion and reduced litigation burdens. Nevertheless, informal systems remain vulnerable to elite capture and unequal participation, particularly when local leaders hold disproportionate influence or when disputants lack social capital (Sukriono et al., 2025; Sulaiman & Satriawan, 2021; Deininger et al., 2021).

Gender implications further complicate the landscape of customary dispute resolution. In many adat and Islam-influenced regimes, women's land rights are variably recognized, and their participation in mediation processes may be constrained by social norms. Women often face barriers to representation, limited legal literacy, and reduced bargaining power within community forums (Singh & Bhatnagar, 2024; Deininger et al., 2021; Toumbourou & Dressler, 2020). Without gender-sensitive safeguards, customary mechanisms may inadvertently reinforce patriarchal inheritance patterns or marginalize secondary land rights. Comparative evidence underscores persistent gender gaps in access to remedy and highlights the need for targeted reforms, including joint titling provisions, representation quotas in customary councils, and training initiatives to enhance women's participation in mediation processes (Khori et al., 2024; Deininger et al., 2021; Toumbourou & Dressler, 2020).

Overall, customary and informal dispute resolution systems remain indispensable components of plural land governance. Their effectiveness rests on cultural legitimacy, restorative orientation, and adaptability to local contexts. Yet their performance is contingent upon integration with formal institutions, transparency in land data, and safeguards against elite capture and gender exclusion. Embedding customary authorities within coherent plural frameworks—while preserving participatory and restorative principles—offers a pathway toward more legitimate and context-sensitive land conflict resolution. Where such integration is achieved, customary mediation can contribute to durable settlements and strengthened social cohesion; where it is absent, fragmentation and perceived injustice may persist, undermining both community harmony and broader governance objectives.

5.2 Formal Judicial and Administrative Systems

Formal judicial and administrative systems constitute a central pillar of land governance, particularly where disputes escalate beyond community-based mediation or involve high-value claims, state actors, or corporate investors. Courts, land commissions, and specialized tribunals are designed to provide authoritative interpretation of statutory law, ensure procedural safeguards, and deliver enforceable decisions. Yet access to these systems remains uneven. While courts are often technically capable of adjudicating complex agrarian cases, they are frequently overwhelmed by caseloads, evidentiary complexity, and overlapping jurisdictional mandates, leading to prolonged delays and declining public trust (Wahid & Sulistiyono, 2025; Arizona & Illiyina, 2024; Sulaiman & Satriawan, 2021). In many contexts, litigants perceive formal processes as slow, costly, and distant from lived realities of customary tenure.

Specialized land courts and alternative adjudication bodies have been introduced in several jurisdictions to address expertise gaps and accelerate dispute resolution. Where land conflicts involve technical cadastral evidence, valuation disputes, or plural legal claims, generalist courts may lack the necessary specialization. Evidence suggests that dedicated land courts or tribunals can improve predictability and speed when supported by clear mandates and adequate resources (Wahid & Sulistiyono, 2025; Arruñada et al., 2022). However, specialization alone does not resolve deeper structural challenges. If underlying legal frameworks remain fragmented or contradictory, even specialized institutions may struggle to produce coherent and legitimate outcomes.

Land tribunals and commissions often face limitations rooted in jurisdictional fragmentation and weak implementation authority. Overlapping mandates between national land agencies, regional commissions, customary land bodies, and administrative courts create uncertainty regarding which institution has final authority (Wahid & Sulistiyono, 2025; Arizona & Illiyina, 2024; Sukirno & Wibawa, 2024; Sahlan et al., 2024). Without effective integration with formal statutory law, tribunal decisions may lack enforceability or be subject to reversal in higher courts. Customary systems can provide local legitimacy, but when their decisions intersect with statutory regimes, enforcement gaps frequently arise (Sukirno & Wibawa, 2024; Afrizal & Berenschot, 2022; Kirabira & Choukroune, 2023). Such fragmentation reduces transparency and may incentivize strategic forum shopping by disputants.

Bureaucratic inefficiencies further complicate formal land administration. Red tape, slow record-keeping, and non-transparent compensation or registration procedures prolong disputes and undermine confidence in governance institutions. Delays in updating land registries, inconsistent cadastral data, and opaque valuation methods create opportunities for rent-seeking and discretionary decision-making (Ferree et al., 2022; Deininger et al., 2021; Chilombo & Horst, 2021). Claimants often face repeated administrative hurdles, unclear documentation requirements, and limited access to timely information. These inefficiencies not only extend disputes but also alienate communities, reinforcing perceptions that formal systems privilege elites or politically connected actors.

Compensation and expropriation processes exemplify these bureaucratic challenges. Where valuation methodologies lack transparency or where consultation processes are superficial, affected communities may perceive formal adjudication as biased or predetermined. Administrative opacity undermines procedural justice and can fuel protest or parallel dispute resolution efforts. Even when courts ultimately provide remedies, prolonged litigation timelines may erode livelihoods and social cohesion in the interim (Deininger et al., 2021). Thus, the legitimacy of formal systems depends not only on substantive rulings but also on efficiency, accessibility, and procedural clarity.

Reforms aimed at enhancing transparency and accountability in formal judicial and administrative systems increasingly emphasize integrated, multi-actor governance. Strengthening coordination among land agencies, courts, and customary authorities can reduce jurisdictional fragmentation and clarify lines of authority (Ferree et al., 2022; Chilombo & Horst, 2021). Formal recognition of customary rights within coherent statutory frameworks may bridge normative divides and enhance enforceability. Technological innovations—such as digitized land registries, participatory mapping, and structured FPIC documentation—can improve legibility and reduce ambiguity in land records (Karambiri et al., 2020; Misbahuddin et al., 2023). However, technological reform must be accompanied by institutional capacity-building and safeguards against exclusion to ensure equitable access.

Accessible dispute resolution pathways are equally critical. Simplified procedures, legal aid services, and decentralized adjudication can reduce barriers for marginalized claimants. Judicial review mechanisms that scrutinize administrative decisions strengthen accountability, particularly in cases involving state-led land deals or corporate concessions. Evidence suggests that transparent land administration reforms and clear grievance mechanisms enhance trust and reduce incentives for extra-legal conflict (Ferree et al., 2022). At the same time, formal systems must remain sensitive to plural legal realities, integrating customary knowledge and participatory inputs where appropriate.

Ultimately, formal judicial and administrative systems occupy a complex position within the land–conflict–justice nexus. They provide enforceable authority and procedural safeguards but face structural constraints stemming from fragmentation, bureaucratic inefficiency, and limited accessibility. Effective reform requires harmonizing statutory law with customary recognition, enhancing transparency in registration and compensation processes, and building institutional capacity to manage complex agrarian disputes. Where these reforms are implemented coherently, formal systems can contribute to predictability, accountability, and conflict mitigation. Where they remain opaque or disconnected from local realities, they risk reinforcing grievances and perpetuating cycles of land-based contestation.

5.3 Hybrid and Alternative Dispute Resolution (ADR) Approaches

Hybrid and alternative dispute resolution (ADR) approaches have emerged as essential bridges between formal judicial systems and customary governance in land disputes. In contexts characterized by legal pluralism, neither statutory courts nor traditional authorities alone can fully address the complexity of overlapping claims, contested legitimacy, and deeply embedded social norms. Hybrid justice mechanisms combine rights-based adjudication with culturally grounded mediation, reflecting processes of institutional bricolage that adapt to layered governance environments (Sukirno & Wibawa, 2024; Ramli et al., 2024; Belew, 2021). Within these arrangements, formal courts retain authority to interpret statutory law and provide enforceable outcomes, while customary or ADR channels offer flexible, socially resonant pathways that are often faster and less costly.

Mediation occupies a central position within hybrid frameworks. Rather than framing disputes as adversarial contests over legal entitlement, mediation redefines them as shared community problems requiring negotiated solutions. This reframing de-escalates tensions and opens space for restorative dialogue, apology, compensation, and mutual recognition (Zaim et al., 2020; Ramli et al., 2024; Belew, 2021). Particularly in disputes involving kinship ties, communal boundaries, or contested customary authority, mediation preserves relationships while clarifying expectations. By embedding negotiation within locally legitimate norms, hybrid mediation reduces the likelihood of protracted litigation and limits the escalation of disputes into violence.

Evidence across comparative contexts suggests that ADR mechanisms can be more equitable than formal courts when power asymmetries are pronounced (Mulu, 2023; Berenschot & Saraswati, 2024; Belew, 2021). Formal courts often privilege documentary evidence, technical cadastral records, and procedural formalities that disadvantage marginalized groups lacking written proof of tenure. ADR processes, by contrast, can incorporate oral histories, communal testimonies, and recognition of collective rights. When inclusively designed, mediation can integrate gender norms and customary expectations, expanding access to justice beyond rigid legal categories. However, this potential depends on careful design. Without safeguards, ADR forums may replicate local hierarchies or entrench elite influence, particularly if facilitators lack independence or if participation is restricted.

Hybrid justice systems function most effectively when coordination between formal and customary institutions is clearly structured rather than left to informal negotiation. Institutional bricolage may involve referral pathways from courts to mediation forums, recognition of customary mediators within statutory frameworks, or codified procedures that align adat principles with national law (Sukirno & Wibawa, 2024). Such arrangements reduce forum shopping and clarify jurisdictional boundaries while preserving contextual sensitivity. By creating formal entry points for customary reasoning, hybrid systems enhance legitimacy without sacrificing enforceability.

Multi-stakeholder platforms (MSPs) represent a broader extension of hybrid ADR approaches. MSPs convene state officials, customary leaders, civil society actors, and private stakeholders to address land disputes through structured dialogue and joint governance mechanisms. Empirical findings indicate that land conflicts decline where inclusive dialogue, transparency, FPIC-like safeguards, and joint monitoring are institutionalized (Sukriono et al., 2025; Berenschot & Saraswati, 2024; Belew, 2021). These platforms foster trust and information sharing, enabling stakeholders to anticipate and negotiate potential disputes before they escalate. By institutionalizing participatory governance within land-use planning and concession processes, MSPs strengthen procedural justice and reduce uncertainty.

Nevertheless, hybrid and multi-stakeholder approaches face persistent tensions. In some contexts, formal legal authority overrides customary rights within collaborative platforms, weakening local legitimacy. In others, participation becomes symbolic, and elite actors dominate decision-making processes (Berenschot & Saraswati, 2024; Ramli et al., 2024; Belew, 2021). Without transparent facilitation, independent oversight, and clear accountability mechanisms, hybrid forums risk becoming arenas of strategic bargaining rather than equitable resolution. Capacity-building for mediators, explicit inclusion of marginalized groups, and monitoring of implementation outcomes are therefore essential to prevent capture.

The promise of hybrid ADR lies in its capacity to reconcile normative diversity with enforceable standards. By integrating statutory safeguards with culturally legitimate mediation practices, hybrid systems address both distributive and procedural dimensions of justice. They reduce litigation burdens on courts, preserve social cohesion, and provide flexible responses to complex disputes that do not fit neatly within singular legal categories. At the same time, hybridization is not a panacea; it requires deliberate design, resource allocation, and commitment to inclusivity.

In plural land governance systems, hybrid and ADR approaches thus represent pragmatic and context-sensitive strategies for conflict mitigation. When inclusive participation, transparency, and clear institutional coordination are embedded, these mechanisms can bridge formal and customary systems, de-escalate disputes, and enhance legitimacy. When poorly designed or inadequately monitored, they may reproduce existing inequities. The effectiveness of hybrid ADR therefore depends not only on procedural innovation but on sustained efforts to align local legitimacy with rights-based accountability.

5.4 Transitional Justice and Land Restitution

In post-conflict settings, land restitution constitutes a central component of rebuilding social trust, restoring livelihoods, and reconstituting legitimate governance. Violent conflict frequently produces mass displacement, destruction of property records, and overlapping claims to housing, land, and property (HLP). Restitution programs are therefore implemented through statutory frameworks, property surveys, and transitional justice (TJ) mechanisms designed to re-establish access to land for dispossessed communities (Cai, 2022; Kirabira & Choukroune, 2023; Jamaluddin et al., 2024). These programs often combine formal adjudication with participatory verification processes, sometimes incorporating customary authorities and FPIC-like safeguards to ensure that return or compensation aligns with community norms and rights recognition.

Statutory restitution schemes typically rely on formal claims procedures, documentary review, and cadastral reconstruction. Property surveys and administrative commissions are tasked with identifying rightful owners, verifying historical occupation, and resolving competing claims. Yet implementation is frequently complicated by overlapping legal regimes and fragmented governance structures. Where statutory law intersects with customary tenure systems, ambiguities arise over which norms govern restitution outcomes (Onyebueke et al., 2020; Zigashane, 2025). Weak enforcement capacity, inadequate land records, and limited documentation of customary rights further hinder effective restitution (Gillett, 2023; Hosen et al., 2020). In many post-conflict environments, the destruction or manipulation of land registries during war deepens uncertainty and creates opportunities for elite capture or opportunistic acquisition.

Transitional justice instruments expand restitution beyond technical property adjudication by linking land rights to broader processes of reconciliation and accountability. Integrating HLP rights within TJ frameworks recognizes that dispossession is often intertwined with ethnic cleansing, political repression, or structural discrimination (Kirabira & Choukroune, 2023). Mechanisms such as truth commissions, reparations programs, and community dialogues address historical grievances while seeking to prevent renewed conflict. Incorporating customary practices within transitional justice processes can enhance legitimacy, particularly where local authorities retain moral authority over land allocation and dispute resolution (Dong et al., 2022; Effendi et al., 2023). Restitution thus becomes both a legal remedy and a symbolic acknowledgment of harm.

Debates persist over how to reconcile formal titling with customary tenure in post-conflict reconstruction. Some restitution programs prioritize individual titling to enhance legal certainty and attract investment, while others emphasize collective recognition of customary territories. Outcomes often depend on institutional hybridity and the legitimacy of actors involved in the process (Ayambire, 2025; Drake & Liunakwalau, 2022). Where negotiations are participatory and procedurally just, hybrid arrangements can harmonize statutory registration with customary verification (Asriyani & Verheijen, 2020; Großmann, 2022). Conversely, when formal law overrides customary claims without adequate consultation, restitution initiatives may reproduce the very grievances they seek to remedy.

Power asymmetries present persistent challenges in land restitution. Post-conflict states may prioritize economic recovery through land-based investment, creating tensions between restitution for displaced populations and development agendas. Corporations or politically connected actors sometimes acquire land during or immediately after conflict, complicating efforts to reverse dispossession (Onyebueke et al., 2020; Zigashane, 2025). Without transparent procedures and independent oversight, restitution processes risk reinforcing inequality. Effective programs therefore require robust safeguards against elite capture and mechanisms to ensure that vulnerable groups—including women, minorities, and displaced households—are not sidelined.

Lessons from comparative post-war contexts emphasize the importance of plural governance and meaningful community participation. Restitution processes that blend FPIC-like consultation, customary dispute resolution, and formal registry systems demonstrate greater legitimacy and durability (Afrizal et al., 2022; Sarfo et al., 2024). Participatory mapping and inclusive verification procedures enhance accuracy while building trust between returnees and host communities. Integrating customary leaders into administrative commissions can bridge normative divides, provided that accountability and gender-sensitive safeguards are maintained (Harris & Honig, 2023). Hybrid institutions that combine statutory authority with locally resonant mediation mechanisms are more likely to produce socially accepted outcomes.

Reparations frameworks further extend restitution by addressing non-material harms and collective memory. Financial compensation, livelihood restoration programs, and symbolic measures—such as memorialization and public acknowledgment—complement property return and help rebuild fractured social relations (Kirabira & Choukroune, 2023). When restitution is linked to broader development planning, including infrastructure reconstruction and land-use reform, it can incentivize investment while protecting community rights (Kurnia et al., 2022). However, economic recovery objectives must be balanced against the imperative of justice; prioritizing growth over equitable redress may entrench post-conflict inequalities.

Evidence also underscores the importance of protecting women's land rights within restitution programs. Post-conflict displacement often exacerbates gender vulnerabilities, particularly where widows or female-headed households lack documentation or face discriminatory inheritance norms. Integrating gender-sensitive safeguards—such as joint titling, representation in restitution bodies, and accessible complaint mechanisms—improves tenure security and reduces the risk of renewed dispossession (Deininger et al., 2021; Harris & Honig, 2023). Ensuring that restitution does not merely restore pre-conflict inequities but advances substantive equality is essential for durable peace.

Overall, transitional justice and land restitution represent intertwined processes aimed at repairing both material loss and social rupture. Their success depends on institutional hybridity, procedural justice, and meaningful participation that bridges statutory and customary systems. Where restitution programs integrate plural governance, transparent administration, and inclusive reparations, they contribute to reconciliation and conflict prevention. Where legal fragmentation, weak enforcement, and power asymmetries persist, restitution may falter, risking renewed contestation. Embedding land restitution within comprehensive transitional justice frameworks is therefore critical for transforming land from a driver of violence into a foundation for sustainable peace.

CHAPTER VI

GOVERNANCE REFORMS, POLICY INTERVENTIONS, AND EMERGING INNOVATIONS

6.1 Land Reform and Tenure Formalization

Land reform and tenure formalization programs have long been advanced as instruments to reduce conflict, enhance tenure security, and promote equitable development. By clarifying boundaries, standardizing documentation, and integrating parcels into cadastral systems, formal titling initiatives are expected to reduce disputes arising from ambiguity and overlapping claims. Empirical evidence indicates that formal titling can diminish boundary conflicts by increasing legibility of rights and enabling landholders to defend claims more effectively (Ferree et al., 2022; Deininger et al., 2021; Asaaga et al., 2020). Clear documentation may also facilitate access to credit and investment, strengthening incentives for smallholders to improve productivity and secure livelihoods. In settings where informal tenure is precarious, titling can provide a degree of legal protection against opportunistic encroachment or arbitrary expropriation.

However, the conflict-mitigating effects of formalization are neither automatic nor uniform. When titling initiatives overlap with strong customary tenure systems or disregard local authority structures, they can provoke new disputes rather than resolve existing ones (Christensen et al., 2021; Noufé, 2023). Tensions frequently emerge where statutory cadastral boundaries fail to reflect customary land allocations or collective rights. In such contexts, formalization may produce competing claims between those holding newly issued certificates and those asserting long-standing customary entitlements. The distinction between legibility and authority becomes critical: while titling enhances administrative clarity, it does not necessarily confer social legitimacy if local norms are bypassed (Ferree et al., 2022; Goyal, 2020). As a result, formalization processes can become arenas of contestation, particularly when local power actors manipulate registration procedures to consolidate control.

The relationship between tenure security and smallholder welfare further illustrates the complexity of reform impacts. Research increasingly emphasizes that tenure security is multi-dimensional, encompassing not only formal documentation but also perceived stability, social recognition, and enforceability (Ferree et al., 2022; Asaaga et al., 2020). In some settings, formal titles enhance security sufficiently to stimulate investment and reduce risk exposure. In others, where customary rights are already socially embedded and widely respected, formal documentation may offer limited additional benefit (Noufé, 2023). Implementation gaps—such as incomplete surveys, weak dispute resolution mechanisms, or lack of transparency—can undermine confidence in new systems. Consequently, titling must be assessed not solely by the issuance of certificates but by its integration with broader governance reforms.

Unintended consequences of land reform highlight further tensions. One concern involves the creation of anticommons scenarios, where excessive fragmentation of rights or unclear delineation of overlapping entitlements blocks productive use (Ferree et al., 2022). Registration processes may inadvertently multiply claimants or formalize contested parcels without resolving underlying disputes. Social stratification can also intensify when elites, chiefs, or politically connected actors capture titling programs to issue informal documents or influence allocation outcomes (Honig, 2022; Takamura et al., 2021). In such circumstances, formalization risks entrenching inequality rather than correcting it. Neoliberal reform agendas that prioritize commodification and market integration may further expose vulnerable groups to dispossession if safeguards are weak or absent (Christensen et al., 2021). These dynamics underscore that formalization is not a neutral technical exercise but a politically embedded process shaped by power asymmetries.

Equity implications are therefore central to evaluating land reform. While titling can empower marginalized groups by strengthening their legal standing, it may also marginalize secondary rights holders—such as women, tenants, or pastoralists—if reforms focus narrowly on individual ownership models (Deininger et al., 2021). Ensuring distributive and procedural justice requires attention to who is included in registration processes and how disputes are adjudicated. Evidence suggests that meaningful participation, transparency, and recognition of customary rights improve outcomes and reduce the likelihood of reform-induced conflict (Ferree et al., 2022). Where community actors are excluded, reforms may exacerbate grievances and trigger resistance.

Policy lessons emerging from comparative research emphasize the importance of hybrid governance arrangements. Successful land reform initiatives tend to incorporate customary authorities within formal systems, employ FPIC-like safeguards, and combine statutory titles with recognized customary entitlements (Ferree et al., 2022; Salay & Day, 2025). Such hybrid models enhance both legibility and legitimacy, reducing friction between normative orders. Participatory mapping and inclusive verification processes can align cadastral records with local understandings of territory, mitigating boundary disputes and strengthening social acceptance.

Ultimately, the impacts of land reform and tenure formalization on conflict and equity depend on institutional design, political context, and implementation quality. Formal titles can reduce disputes and stimulate investment when embedded within transparent, inclusive governance frameworks. Yet when reforms ignore local authority structures, overlook secondary rights, or privilege market logics over social justice, they may generate new conflicts and deepen inequality. Land formalization thus represents a double-edged instrument within the land–conflict–justice nexus: capable of clarifying rights and enhancing security, but equally capable of provoking contestation if legitimacy and equity are not carefully safeguarded.

6.2 Community Land Recognition and Collective Rights

Legal recognition of Indigenous and community land systems has emerged as a central reform pathway within contemporary land governance, particularly in contexts marked by legal pluralism and historical dispossession. Recognizing collective tenure can reduce conflict by clarifying territorial boundaries, strengthening tenure security, and fostering cooperative governance between Indigenous groups and the state. Where collective rights are formally acknowledged, unilateral expropriation becomes more difficult, and negotiated settlements gain institutional grounding (Nindyatmoko et al., 2022; Geyer, 2024; Karambiri et al., 2020). Recognition processes that document customary territories and integrate them into national legal systems enhance both legibility and legitimacy, thereby mitigating boundary disputes and jurisdictional ambiguity.

However, recognition is not uniformly transformative. In contexts where recognition remains partial, ambiguous, or politically contested, tensions persist due to competing legitimacies and overlapping authorities (Matteo, 2023; Iswanto et al., 2022). State agencies may acknowledge collective land rights in principle while retaining discretionary control over subsoil resources, infrastructure corridors, or conservation zones. Such layered authority structures can produce uncertainty regarding the scope of community autonomy. Where statutory and customary norms are not harmonized, formal recognition may coexist with ongoing disputes over implementation, enforcement, or benefit-sharing.

Reforms aimed at strengthening Indigenous territorial rights have yielded varied outcomes across comparative settings. In some cases, collective titling and territorial demarcation have improved tenure security and signaled stability to investors and development partners. By establishing clear governance structures and recognized leadership, these reforms can enhance community capacity to negotiate with external actors (Karambiri et al., 2020). Yet in other contexts, reforms have reallocated rights internally or reframed ownership categories in ways that generate new power asymmetries. Institutional bricolage processes—where actors adapt or reinterpret rules—may produce unintended consequences, including anticommons situations or elite capture within communities (Claessens et al., 2021; Mwanza et al., 2024; Takamura et al., 2021). Thus, recognition does not automatically eliminate contestation; it reshapes it within new institutional configurations.

The intersection of collective land rights with state sovereignty frequently hinges on tensions between legality and legitimacy. Formal titling can improve legibility for national planning and investment, offering clear documentation of collective boundaries. Yet when such processes are not co-designed with communities, they may undermine customary authority or impose governance models that conflict with local norms (Christensen et al., 2021; Salay & Day, 2025; Ferree et al., 2022). The challenge lies in balancing the state's interest in standardized administration with communities' claims to self-determination and culturally embedded land stewardship. Where recognition frameworks respect participatory principles and incorporate customary institutions into formal decision-making, legitimacy tends to strengthen.

Community land certification programs illustrate both the promise and the risks of collective recognition. Evidence suggests that certification strengthens tenure security when embedded within participatory governance arrangements and supported by FPIC-like processes that ensure informed consent and ongoing dialogue (Tsering, 2025; Mujiburohman et al., 2024). Participatory mapping, transparent boundary verification, and inclusive dispute resolution mechanisms contribute to durable recognition. Conversely, technocratic or top-down implementation may exacerbate distrust, particularly if communities perceive reforms as instruments of state consolidation rather than empowerment (Zikargie, 2025; Ismi & Hasanah, 2023). Effective certification therefore depends not only on legal enactment but on procedural justice and meaningful community engagement.

Overall, community land recognition and collective rights reforms represent critical instruments for advancing equity and conflict mitigation within plural governance systems. When recognition is comprehensive, participatory, and institutionally integrated, it can reduce unilateral dispossession and facilitate negotiated development pathways. Where recognition remains partial, poorly implemented, or disconnected from customary authority, tensions endure. Embedding collective rights within hybrid governance frameworks that align statutory law with customary legitimacy is therefore essential to transforming community land recognition into a durable foundation for justice and sustainable land governance.

6.3 Digitalization and Land Administration Technologies

Digitalization has become a prominent feature of contemporary land administration reform, with governments increasingly adopting digital registries, blockchain systems, and GIS-based mapping to enhance transparency and reduce disputes. These technologies are often promoted as tools to improve legibility, streamline registration, and strengthen public trust. Evidence suggests that digital land registration can enhance transparency and reduce conflicts when it produces accessible, verifiable records and enables real-time updates of transactions and boundary changes (Mwanza et al., 2024; Deininger et al., 2021; Afrizal & Berenschot, 2022; Sumarni et al., 2023). By reducing opportunities for document tampering and bureaucratic delay, digital systems may limit rent-seeking and clarify chains of title.

However, the conflict-reducing potential of digital registries depends heavily on governance design. Legal pluralism presents particular challenges where customary and statutory systems coexist. Digital records that privilege statutory titles without adequately integrating customary claims may exacerbate formal–informal tensions rather than resolve them (Deininger et al., 2021; Afrizal & Berenschot, 2022). In contexts where informal transactions or communal tenure remain prevalent, digitization may formalize only a subset of claims, leaving others vulnerable. Thus, while digital systems improve administrative clarity, they do not automatically reconcile competing normative frameworks.

Blockchain-enabled registries are frequently presented as innovations capable of enhancing tamper-resistance and public traceability. By creating decentralized, immutable records, blockchain technologies aim to reduce corruption and strengthen trust in land transactions (Deininger et al., 2021; Mwanza et al., 2024; Ferree et al., 2022). Yet these systems may transfer risk to users if governance safeguards are weak. Where communities lack meaningful participation, informed consent, or technical literacy, blockchain-based systems risk entrenching exclusion. In plural legal environments, immutable digital entries may freeze contested claims before they are socially validated, complicating dispute resolution rather than simplifying it.

GIS-based mapping has demonstrated significant potential to improve boundary visibility and reduce boundary-related disputes. Accurate spatial data can clarify parcel demarcation, identify overlaps, and facilitate coordinated land-use planning (Deininger et al., 2021; Afrizal & Berenschot, 2022; Sumarni et al., 2023). Where boundaries are central to claims—particularly in peri-urban expansion or resource-rich areas—GIS tools can provide objective reference points that reduce ambiguity. Nevertheless, mapping does not automatically resolve conflicts rooted in competing historical narratives or divergent customary and statutory understandings of territory. Spatial clarity must be complemented by participatory verification processes to ensure legitimacy.

Inclusivity remains a critical concern in digital land governance. Digital systems risk excluding marginalized groups who lack internet access, digital literacy, or influence in governance processes. Without deliberate design to ensure accessibility, technological reform may widen rather than narrow disparities (Toh et al., 2023; Tedla & Mekonen, 2023; Mwanza et al., 2024). Participatory design, multi-stakeholder oversight, and user-friendly grievance mechanisms are therefore essential to prevent digital exclusion. Embedding FPIC-like safeguards and community consultation in digitalization initiatives enhances both procedural justice and trust.

In contexts where boundaries are co-governed by state and customary authorities, digital legibility can simultaneously enable and reconfigure conflict. Transparent records may strengthen claims and facilitate negotiation, but they can also consolidate state authority or marginalize customary institutions if integration is uneven (Gyan, 2025; Ubink & Almeida, 2023; Arruñada et al., 2022; Ferree et al., 2022). Understanding plural governance dynamics is therefore crucial to avoid new forms of dispossession arising from technologically driven reform.

Overall, digital land administration technologies offer significant opportunities to enhance transparency, reduce bureaucratic inefficiency, and clarify boundaries. Yet their capacity to mitigate conflict depends on inclusive governance, integration with customary systems, and safeguards against exclusion. Digitalization is not a substitute for institutional reform; rather, it must be embedded within participatory, rights-based frameworks to ensure that technological innovation advances equity and durable dispute reduction within the land–conflict–justice nexus.

6.4 Rights-Based and Participatory Governance Models

Rights-based and participatory governance models have gained prominence as corrective responses to technocratic and exclusionary land reforms. These approaches foreground citizen engagement, legal empowerment, and collective rights recognition as central pillars of conflict mitigation and equitable land administration. Rather than treating land governance as a purely administrative exercise, participatory models situate it within broader struggles over legitimacy, accountability, and justice.

Participatory mapping represents one of the most widely adopted instruments within this paradigm. When embedded in formal–customary co-governance arrangements, participatory mapping can reduce land conflict by aligning competing claims, improving spatial data accuracy, and strengthening local legitimacy (Zaim et al., 2020; Seko & Soa, 2025). Evidence from village-level systems, including Bengkulu cases and Bengkok/Bengko land arrangements, demonstrates that citizen involvement in land-use planning enhances collective understanding of boundaries and tenure status (Toh et al., 2023; Day, 2023). By integrating local knowledge with administrative records, participatory mapping fosters mutual recognition between communities and state authorities. However, participatory processes do not automatically guarantee equitable outcomes. Where enforcement mechanisms are weak or where elite actors dominate consultations, mapping initiatives may be co-opted, producing mixed or even adverse effects (Toh et al., 2023; Day, 2023; Mireku et al., 2021). The quality of facilitation, transparency of data use, and follow-through by authorities determine whether participation translates into durable dispute reduction.

Legal empowerment complements participatory mapping by equipping communities with the knowledge, tools, and procedural access necessary to claim and defend land rights. Programs that enhance rights awareness, provide legal aid, and strengthen access to grievance mechanisms improve transparency in government and corporate land dealings (Prabu et al., 2022; Yusuf et al., 2025; Day, 2023; Abonga et al., 2024). When communities understand statutory protections and procedural avenues, they are better positioned to challenge unlawful expropriation or inequitable compensation. Recognition of FPIC, customary courts, and plural legal mechanisms further strengthens procedural influence, allowing communities to engage on more equal footing with state and private actors (Prabu et al., 2022; Wiratraman, 2025; Chilombo & Horst, 2021; Putri & Noer, 2023). Legal empowerment thus shifts land governance from passive administration to active rights-claiming.

Human rights frameworks provide normative grounding for participatory governance. By anchoring land governance within rights to housing, culture, livelihood, and non-discrimination, these frameworks encourage reforms oriented toward inclusion and accountability (Prabu et al., 2022; Errico & Claeys, 2020). Rights-based approaches emphasize that land disputes are not merely technical disagreements but often implicate fundamental human entitlements. Yet tensions arise where rights protections are selectively applied or domesticated to favor development objectives over community autonomy (Chilombo & Horst, 2021; Abdulgani & Savitri, 2025; Abonga et al., 2024). Ensuring consistency between rights rhetoric and implementation remains a central challenge.

Procedural justice improves when participatory land governance is institutionalized through clear rules, accessible dispute mechanisms, and independent oversight. Evidence from Indonesia and other comparative settings indicates that structured participation—supported by transparent guidelines and monitoring—enhances trust and reduces escalation (Zaim et al., 2020; Seko & Soa, 2025). Conversely, informal or ad hoc participation without enforceable commitments may fail to alter power asymmetries (Day, 2023; Putri & Noer, 2023). Embedding participatory governance within formal administrative processes, while preserving space for customary deliberation, strengthens both legitimacy and accountability.

Grassroots advocacy initiatives further reinforce rights-based governance by mobilizing collective action and amplifying marginalized voices. Civil society organizations often facilitate community mapping, legal literacy campaigns, and policy dialogue, bridging gaps between local claims and national reform agendas (Abonga et al., 2024). Through advocacy, communities can influence legislative reform, monitor implementation, and hold authorities accountable. However, sustained impact depends on institutional receptiveness and the capacity of advocacy networks to navigate political constraints.

Overall, rights-based and participatory governance models offer pathways to reconcile plural legal systems, reduce conflict, and advance equity. When participatory mapping, legal empowerment, and human rights frameworks are integrated into coherent institutional designs, they enhance procedural justice and strengthen collective tenure security. Yet participation must be genuine, inclusive, and supported by enforceable safeguards to avoid tokenism or elite capture. Embedding these models within broader land reform strategies ensures that governance innovations contribute not only to administrative efficiency but to substantive justice within the land–conflict–justice nexus.

CHAPTER VII

CONCLUDING REMARKS

The land–conflict–justice nexus through interconnected analytical lenses spanning political economy, legal pluralism, justice theory, environmental change, identity politics, and governance reform. Across rural, peri-urban, and post-conflict settings, land emerges not merely as a material asset but as a political, economic, and symbolic resource that structures authority, belonging, and social hierarchy. Conflicts over land are rarely reducible to boundary disputes alone; they reflect deeper tensions over recognition, distribution, procedural fairness, and historical redress.

The analysis demonstrates that tenure insecurity and overlapping claims constitute recurring drivers of dispute. Where cadastral weaknesses, legal fragmentation, and elite capture undermine clarity, land becomes a site of strategic contestation. Large-scale land acquisitions, urban expansion, and climate-induced resource pressures intensify these dynamics, particularly when governance institutions fail to align formal and customary regimes. In identity-based and ethno-political contexts, land serves as a proxy for sovereignty and memory, linking territorial claims to broader struggles over citizenship and state legitimacy. Gendered dimensions further reveal how structural inequality permeates land governance, shaping both the origins and outcomes of disputes.

Justice frameworks provide a critical lens for evaluating governance responses. Distributive justice concerns the allocation of land benefits and burdens; procedural justice addresses participation, transparency, and accountability; recognition justice demands acknowledgment of Indigenous and customary rights; and restorative justice emphasizes reconciliation and social repair. The review underscores that formal titling alone cannot deliver equitable outcomes unless embedded within inclusive and participatory processes. Hybrid governance arrangements—combining statutory authority with customary legitimacy—recur as promising yet context-dependent solutions.

Dispute resolution mechanisms illustrate the importance of institutional integration. Customary and informal mediation systems often deliver culturally resonant and restorative outcomes, while formal courts and administrative bodies provide enforceable authority. Hybrid ADR approaches and multi-stakeholder platforms bridge these spheres, demonstrating potential to reduce escalation when designed with transparency and inclusive safeguards. Transitional justice and land restitution in post-conflict settings further highlight the necessity of linking material redress with memory, reparations, and durable institutional reform.

Reform pathways explored in this review—land formalization, community land recognition, digitalization, and rights-based governance—offer both opportunities and risks. Formalization can clarify rights and stimulate investment, yet may generate new conflicts if customary claims are marginalized. Recognition of collective rights can reduce unilateral dispossession but requires careful negotiation of legality and legitimacy. Digital technologies enhance transparency and boundary clarity, though they risk exclusion if not embedded in participatory frameworks. Participatory mapping, legal empowerment, and grassroots advocacy demonstrate that procedural inclusion is central to conflict mitigation and equitable governance.

Taken together, the evidence suggests that durable land justice depends on plural, hybrid, and context-sensitive governance models. Effective reform must integrate customary institutions, statutory law, technological innovation, and human rights principles within coherent and accountable frameworks. Participation, transparency, and recognition are not ancillary features but foundational conditions for reducing conflict and strengthening legitimacy. Ultimately, transforming land from a recurrent driver of violence into a foundation for equitable development requires sustained institutional commitment, attention to power asymmetries, and alignment between administrative legibility and social legitimacy

References

Abdulgani, F. and Savitri, L. (2025). State, Capital and Coercion in Indonesia's Food Estates. *Journal of Agrarian Change, 25*(4). https://doi.org/10.1111/joac.70031

Abdo, M. (2023). Role of International Institutions in Ethiopia's Rural Land Policy. *Mizan Law Review, 17*(2), 343–378. https://doi.org/10.4314/mlr.v17i2.5

Abonga, F., Atingo, J., Awachango, J., Denis, A., Hopwood, J., James, O., ... & Okello, J. (2024). Collaborative Autoethnography and Reclaiming an African Episteme: Investigating "Customary" Ownership of Natural Resources. *African Studies Review, 67*(2), 416–430. https://doi.org/10.1017/asr.2023.112

Afrizal, A. (2022). Analysing the effectiveness of the roundtable on sustainable palm oil's Free, Prior and Informed Consent policy to respect customary land rights. *Journal of International Development, 35*(5), 761–780. https://doi.org/10.1002/jid.3700

Afrizal, A. and Berenschot, W. (2022). Land-Use Change Conflicts and Anti-Corporate Activism in Indonesia: A Review Essay. *Journal of East Asian Studies, 22*(2), 333–356. https://doi.org/10.1017/jea.2022.12

Akhtar, Z. (2023). Indigenous storytelling and admissibility in common law courts: Developing the protocols for the reception theory of evidence. *The International Journal of Evidence & Proof, 27*(2), 143–166. https://doi.org/10.1177/13657127231155922

Arruñada, B., Fabbri, M., & Faure, M. (2022). Land Titling and Litigation. *The Journal of Law and Economics, 65*(1), 131–156. https://doi.org/10.1086/716756

Asaaga, F., Hirons, M., & Malhi, Y. (2020). Questioning the link between tenure security and sustainable land management in cocoa landscapes in Ghana. *World Development, 130*, 104913. https://doi.org/10.1016/j.worlddev.2020.104913

Ayambire, R. (2025). Rethinking planning in post-colonial cities: Institutional hybridity, power, and conflict. *Planning Theory, 25*(1), 28–47. https://doi.org/10.1177/14730952251359052

Berenschot, W. and Saraswati, N. (2024). Discourses of Land Conflicts in Indonesia. *Development and Change, 55*(6), 1182–1205. https://doi.org/10.1111/dech.12865

Boamah, E. and Amoako, C. (2019). Planning by (mis)rule of laws: The idiom and dilemma of planning within Ghana's dual legal land systems. *Environment and Planning C: Politics and Space, 38*(1), 97–115. https://doi.org/10.1177/2399654419855400

Christensen, D., Hartman, A., & Samii, C. (2021). Legibility and External Investment: An Institutional Natural Experiment in Liberia. *International Organization, 75*(4), 1087–1108. https://doi.org/10.1017/s0020818321000187

Claessens, K., Bisoka, A., & Ansoms, A. (2021). Rethinking Communal Land Governance in the Great Lakes Region of Central Africa. *Progress in Development Studies, 21*(2), 144–160. https://doi.org/10.1177/14649934211006553

Day, J. (2023). CITY OF NON-EQUIVALENTS: Making, Maintaining and Disrupting Customary Attachments to Land in Port Vila, Vanuatu. *International Journal of Urban and Regional Research, 47*(6), 995–1012. https://doi.org/10.1111/1468-2427.13208

Day, J., Wewerinke-Singh, M., & Price, S. (2020). Eviction is not a disaster. *Development Policy Review, 39*(1), 103–120. https://doi.org/10.1111/dpr.12460

Deininger, K., Xia, F., Kilic, T., & Moylan, H. (2021). Investment impacts of gendered land rights in customary tenure systems: Substantive and methodological insights from Malawi. *World Development, 147,* 105654. https://doi.org/10.1016/j.worlddev.2021.105654

Effendi, M., Nasution, M., Harahap, R., & Amin, M. (2023). Model for Ulayat Land Conflict Resolution in North Sumatra, Indonesia. *International Journal of Sustainable Development and Planning, 18*(7), 2177–2182. https://doi.org/10.18280/ijsdp.180721

Errico, S. and Claeys, P. (2020). Human Rights and the Commons: Exploring Approaches to the Governance of Land and Natural Resources beyond Indigenous Peoples' Rights. The Case of Peasants. *International Journal on Minority and Group Rights, 27*(1), 1–33. https://doi.org/10.1163/15718115-02604123

Ferree, K., Honig, L., Lust, E., & Phillips, M. (2022). Land and Legibility: When Do Citizens Expect Secure Property Rights in Weak States? *American Political Science Review, 117*(1), 42–58. https://doi.org/10.1017/s0003055422000417

Geyer, H. (2024). Customary land management systems and urban planning in peri-urban informal settlements. *Urban Studies,* 62(2), 310–327. https://doi.org/10.1177/00420980241253790

Geyer, H. (2024). ZONING AND THE 'RIGHT' CITY: The Challenges of Zoning in the Global South and Possibilities for Unzoning Informality. *International Journal of Urban and Regional Research, 48*(5), 877–893. https://doi.org/10.1111/1468-2427.13270

Goyal, A. (2020). Customary Land-Tenure and the Poor: A Study of Jharkhand and Meghalaya. *Social Change, 50*(3), 430–446. https://doi.org/10.1177/0049085720951178

Gyan, A. (2025). Persistent Shadows of Legal Pluralism: Digital Land Governance and Cyclical Land Administration Setbacks in Ghana. *Africa Spectrum*. https://doi.org/10.1177/00020397251361944

Honig, L. (2022). The Power of the Pen: Informal Property Rights Documents in Zambia. *African Affairs, 121*(482), 81–107. https://doi.org/10.1093/afraf/adab034

Karambiri, M., Brockhaus, M., Sehring, J., & Degrande, A. (2020). 'We Are Not Bad People'—Bricolage and the Rise of Community Forest Institutions in Burkina Faso. *International Journal of the Commons, 14*(1), 525–538. https://doi.org/10.5334/ijc.1061

Matteo, F. (2023). Between international norms and land politics: the role of translocal actors in Kenyan arenas of land policy reform. *The Journal of Modern African Studies, 61*(4), 495–520. https://doi.org/10.1017/s0022278x23000216

Mintah, K., Baako, K., Kavaarpuo, G., & Otchere, G. (2020). Skin lands in Ghana and application of blockchain technology for acquisition and title registration. *Journal of Property Planning and Environmental Law, 12*(2), 147–169. https://doi.org/10.1108/jppel-12-2019-0062

Mujiburohman, D., Andari, D., Junarto, R., & Mujiati, M. (2024). The Patterns of Ownership and the Registration of Customary Land in Manggarai Regency, Indonesia. *Jurnal Ilmiah Peuradeun, 12*(1), 293–314. https://doi.org/10.26811/peuradeun.v12i1.969

Mwanza, D., Munshifwa, E., & Kalaba, F. (2024). Perceived Land Scarcity and Its Effects on Traditional Tenure Rights in Rural Zambia. *Journal of Asian and African Studies, 60*(5), 3012–3029. https://doi.org/10.1177/00219096231225951

Nindyatmoko, A., Setyowati, K., & Haryanti, R. (2022). Collaboration after Conflict: A Lesson from Collaborative Action in Customary Land Tenure Conflicts in Lombok, Indonesia. *Forest and Society, 6*(1), 294–310. https://doi.org/10.24259/fs.v6i1.14005

Noufé, T. (2023). Impact of land tenure security through customary law on agricultural productivity in Burkina Faso. *Land Use Policy, 134,* 106907. https://doi.org/10.1016/j.landusepol.2023.106907

Prabu, N., Rumiartha, B., Luh, N., Astariyani, N., Agung, A., & Indradewi, S. (2022). Human Rights of Indigenous People in Indonesia: A Constitutional Approach. *Journal of East Asia and International Law, 15*(2), 395–402. https://doi.org/10.14330/jeail.2022.15.2.10

Salay, S. and Day, J. (2025). Overlapping Land Tenure Stories: Ambiguity in Port Vila's Urban Precarity. *City & Society, 37*(1). https://doi.org/10.1111/ciso.70009

Sumarni, S., Wijaya, M., & Sugiana, A. (2023). Safeguarding Indigenous Rights and Territories: Integrating Dayak Ngaju Wisdom in Peatland Ecosystem Management. *Udayana Journal of Law and Culture, 7*(2), 121. https://doi.org/10.24843/ujlc.2023.v07.i02.p01

Takamura, G., Nishide, T., Kanazawa, Y., & Hayashi, M. (2021). Bundle of Rights Reversed: Anticommons in a Japanese Common Property Forest Due to Legalization. *International Journal of the Commons, 15*(1), 259–275. https://doi.org/10.5334/ijc.1080

Tedla, W. and Mekonen, K. (2023). Inheritance-induced familial disputes in north-west Ethiopia. *Humanities and Social Sciences Communications, 10*(1). https://doi.org/10.1057/s41599-023-01558-5

Toh, M., Choon, T., Looi, K., Tan, W., Ujang, U., Chin, T., ... & Kathitasapathy, S. (2023). Towards "Good" Native Land Governance. *International Indigenous Policy Journal, 14*(1). https://doi.org/10.18584/iipj.2023.14.1.13873

Ubink, J. and Almeida, B. (2023). Local Self-Governance and the State in South Sudan. *Politics and Governance, 11*(2), 357–367. https://doi.org/10.17645/pag.v11i2.6488

Wiratraman, H. (2025). Cultural Expertise and the Social Justice Defense of Indigenous Peoples Rights in the Indonesian Constitutional Court. *Constitutional Review, 11*(2), 299–339. https://doi.org/10.31078/consrev1122

Zaim, Z., Rudiarto, I., Buchori, I., & Wahyudi, A. (2020). Community Participation Pattern in Communal Village Land Utilization. *International Review for Spatial Planning and Sustainable Development, 8*(3), 54–67. https://doi.org/10.14246/irspsd.8.3_54

Zikargie, Y. (2025). Contesting Modernist Land Development. *Africa Review, 18*(1), 81–105. https://doi.org/10.1163/09744061-bja10321

SYNOPSIS

Land, Conflict & Justice: Governance, Power, and Pathways to Equitable Resolution offers a comprehensive analysis of the complex relationship between land, conflict, and justice within contemporary governance frameworks. Grounded in the understanding that land is not merely an economic asset but also a source of identity, livelihood, cultural meaning, and political legitimacy, the book examines how land issues frequently become arenas of power struggles, structural inequality, and tensions between statutory and customary legal systems. The opening chapters develop a conceptual foundation for understanding the land–conflict nexus, highlighting the role of legal pluralism in shaping competing claims, authority, and legitimacy. The discussion then turns to land reform and tenure formalization, demonstrating how titling and cadastral reforms can reduce disputes and enhance tenure security, while also generating new conflicts when they intersect with customary systems or reinforce local power asymmetries.

Subsequent chapters explore the legal recognition of collective and Indigenous land rights as both a legal and political process. The book emphasizes the importance of social legitimacy, meaningful participation, and the integration of formal institutions with community-based governance in advancing equitable land justice. It also critically examines the digital transformation of land administration—such as digital registries, GIS mapping, and blockchain technologies—assessing their potential to improve transparency and dispute resolution while cautioning against risks of exclusion and new forms of dispossession.

In its concluding sections, the book discusses rights-based and participatory governance models, including participatory mapping, legal empowerment, and community-based dispute resolution mechanisms. Overall, this volume presents an interdisciplinary and reflective framework that advocates for hybrid governance approaches—integrating procedural justice, recognition of collective rights, and inclusive institutions—as essential pathways toward more equitable and sustainable land conflict resolution.

BIOGRAPHY AUTHOR

Dr. Safrin Salam, S.H., M.H., was born in Baubau on February 1, 1990. He completed his Doctoral Degree (S3) in Law at the Faculty of Law, Hasanuddin University, Makassar, in 2022. His academic focus centers on customary law, land law, agrarian reform, and legal pluralism in Indonesia.

He began his academic career in 2016 as a permanent lecturer at the Faculty of Law, Universitas Muhammadiyah Buton. Since the same year, he has served as Editor-in-Chief of *Jurnal Hukum Volkgeist*, contributing to the development of legal scholarship and academic publication management. He is also an active reviewer for several law journals in Indonesia. In his teaching role, he is responsible for the Customary Law course and is actively involved in advancing the study and institutional development of customary law. He is a board member of the Indonesian Association of Customary Law Lecturers (APHA). His scholarly publications include national works such as *Legal Protection of Indigenous Peoples over Customary Forests* (2015), *Legal Certainty in the Issuance of Communal Land Certificates as an Implementation of Agrarian Reform*, and *Marriage Dispensation for Underage Children: Perspectives of Customary Law, State Law, and Islamic Law*. At the international level, his publications include *Land Registry: Communal Rights Certificate and the Problems in Indonesia* (2018) and *Corporate Legal Responsibility Against Environmental Damage* (2019), among others.

Publisher: Eliva Press Global Ltd

Email: info@elivapress.com

www.ingramcontent.com/pod-product-compliance
Lightning Source LLC
LaVergne TN
LVHW022322200926
848481LV00004B/1399
* 9 7 8 9 9 9 9 3 3 8 4 9 3 *